French Impressions

French Impressions

*...of the land, the life and lives of
people of south west France*

Jillian Taberner

© Jillian Taberner 2009

Published by Brubooks 2009

ISBN 978-0-9561881-0-6

Cover design by Clare Brayshaw

Prepared by:

York Publishing Services Ltd,
64 Hallfield Road,
Layerthorpe,
York
YO31 7ZQ
Telephone 01904 431213

www.yps-publishing.co.uk

Acknowledgement

I would like to thank my husband, John, who went along with my dream to have a house in France. Thank you for all your help; proofreading, checking facts, grammar and spelling, to say nothing of your advice and support. Love to my children Anna, Carey and Richard (who love my house in France almost as much as I do) with thanks for your encouragement and belief in me. Thank you to my dear friend Hilde for the suggestion of the title, which had eluded me for sometime, also thanks to all those who gave me photographs.

I would also like to acknowledge the advice and information given out by local tourist offices, including answering my questions and indicating the key items of interest in their area.

Last but not least, I would like to thank the people who appear in this book who gave me their time and willingly took me into their confidence and talked about their lives.

Foreword

This book is about my impressions of a particular corner of south west France, centred on the three departments Lot et Garonne, Tarn et Garonne and the Lot. It draws parallels between these three departments and highlights their differences. It explores to some extent the history and culture of the three areas and describes scenery, places of interest and tourist attractions to appeal to both adults and children.

I tell you about some good restaurants worth visiting where the children can enjoy a delicious *crêpe* with a choice of delicious toppings or fillings. I include some typical menus from some of the restaurants to entice the adults to visit.

It is a copiously illustrated narrative with stories of strong human interest. The people featured in this book share their daily working lives with the reader, whether they were born here or came here later in life. They tell of their occupations and how they came to use their latent talents, or learn new skills, and subsequently do what they now believe was their vocation.

The book also includes favourite recipes of some of these people and some of my own, which I have practised and modified to family preferences. A recipe is a formula with exact amounts which give consistent results but recipes change hands and therefore change character, sometimes for the better, sometimes for the worse! All you need is common sense, a love of cooking, a degree of artistry and experiment, which makes cooking exciting. Each cook brings their own particular expertise to a recipe and so I urge you to take the recipes and, with your knowledge, add your own level of imagination.

Contents

PART 3

Life stories:

RECIPES

Recipes occur throughout the text; mostly in the sections featuring individuals who have given them, along with some of my own.

Introduction

'Connaître une région, c'est connaître la vie des gens qui l'ont batie.'

"To get to know a region one must first know the people who have built it."

That is to say, to know the fundamental nature of the people who through tradition, beliefs and customs have created a life; a life surrounded by a specific terrain, who have adapted to the particular climate, who have become the essence of the place.

This is how I have come to know the area around the conjunction of three departmental boundaries in the south west of France.

Mainland France is divided into 96 departments, but though similar to counties in the United Kingdom, they have more autonomy. It was in 1790, after the beginning of the French Revolution, that the provinces were divided into departments. Generally, they were named after a mountain or river.

If you draw a circle, with a radius of about 25 kilometres around the meeting point of the borders of the three departments of the Lot, the Lot et Garonne and the Tarn et Garonne, you will find these three boundaries come together like three running legs. If it were not for

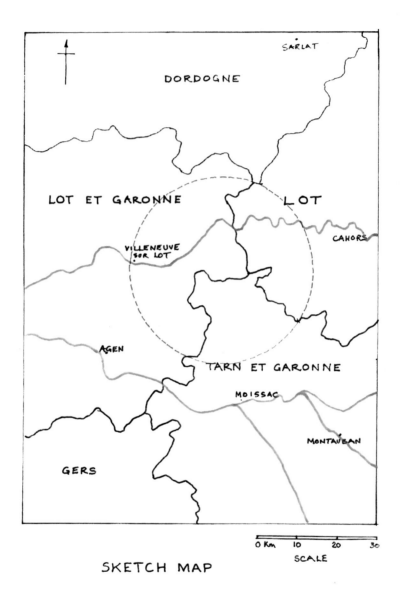

SKETCH MAP

an area of land in the north east corner of the Tarn et Garonne, with a finger pushing up into the Lot, these three legs would almost join at the hip so to speak, in the centre of this circle. At one time, this corner of land belonged to Agen, which is in the Lot et Garonne, and in 1911 papers were formally drawn up to straighten out the border in this area. It seems strange but the papers were 'lost' and the area has stayed in the Tarn et Garonne. Nevertheless, the three boundaries intersect to form three more or less triangular sections, widening out into the main body of each of the departments.

It is through the people I have met here, in the corners of these three departments that I have come to know this region.

Crossing the boundaries within this circle between one department and another there is no dramatic change of scenery, only the departmental sign proclaiming you are now in a different territory. These signs each proudly display the departmental logo, often with a complimentary tag, to remind you of the beauty of the scenery, the delights of the region and the historic sights not to be missed.

Gradually as one travels deeper into each department the scenery does change as the geography of the land alters. The culture and traditions vary, and along with them the life style, and people's loyalty to their own region becomes apparent. Just as in Britain, or any other country for that matter, the inhabitants of one area believe in its superiority over the neighbouring one. But sometimes there's more than an allegiance to a particular department; it becomes a form of rivalry.

It must be the exacting administrative system of the departmental divisions in France which make it impossible to buy a postcard of a Tarn et Garonne scene in a shop in Lot et Garonne!

My first experience of this was at the local shop in Dausse, a village near to Valeilles where I have a house. It's an Aladdin's cave; it sells bread, groceries, vegetables and fruit, newspapers, tobacco, delicatessen, toys, games, even clothes, and of course postcards. Dausse lies on the northern side of the small river known as Le Moulinet, about one kilometre from Valeilles. The rub is - Le Moulinet is the departmental boundary.

My request for postcards of Valeilles and its surroundings was greeted with the surprised response;

'Oh no, Madame, that's another department!'

The same sort of surprised reaction occurred when shopping in Villeneuve-sur-Lot, giving my address for delivery of goods;

'Oh, you live there, do you?' Another country!

When I crossed that small river I didn't need a passport but I was almost made to feel as though I did. It seemed as though I had passed between two different lands even though the inhabitants spoke the same language. In reality the people generally go about their daily lives, passing to and fro without heed to a border which is physically invisible and psychologically imperceptible until...a regulation, a competition, a football match, even buying a postcard, and then they belong to one department or the other.

The three departments featured in this book have a major feature in common – notably a river, each one long, wide and renowned for the beautiful scenery along its course. Each department boasts its particular, long historic traditions, with churches and houses of significant architectural interest, its sights and customs. What they also have in common is their love of food – their gastronomic delights, differing slightly as you move from one to the other; farm produce, duck, cheeses, fruit, vegetables, grapes and of course wine.

You will see from time to time throughout this area the soubriquet 'Pays de Serres'. It puzzled me for quite a while – the word 'serre' means either a greenhouse, or a talon or claw. But what did this countryside have to do with either of those meanings? It was a French friend who let me into the secret. It is a geographical area, which viewed from the air gives the impression of having been grooved, ridged, by the claws of a bird of prey. It occurs along the chalk plateau and enclosed valleys facing north east/south west, which stretch to the north as far as Cahors in the Lot and to the south to Montaigu de Quercy in Tarn et Garonne. The area stretches into the Lot et Garonne too, as far as Agen to the south and west through the *contrée,* a region within the Lot et Garonne department known as the *Confluent.*

Another geographical area, which from an administrative point of view is no longer applied, is that of Quercy. It is one of the former regions of France, but the name is still used to describe the land, its customs, and its culture that fall within its boundaries.

Throughout this south west corner of France the most well-known fare is *foie gras;* you cannot travel more than a kilometre or two without seeing a sign proclaiming its availability. Sometimes it's a large, flashy hoarding on the roadside with detailed instructions to help you find the place. Sometimes it's a small hand-written notice on an old piece of wood hammered into a post at the end of a long drive. Wherever you buy it – it's good. Very good! Fear not, the goose is a greedy creature and no matter what you may hear about 'force feeding', the geese are very willing to eat!

And then of course, equally well known, there's duck; *magret* – served succulent and red; *confit* – the duck leg preserved in fat; *manchons* – preserved wings; and *aiguillettes* – slices of fine lean meat from the side of the duck.

Each department has its own speciality, which may be a gastronomic treat or an area of expertise. In both the Tarn et Garonne and the Lot et Garonne you will find prunes; *Pruneaux d'Agenais,* the soft, dark, juicy prunes made from the plums grown abundantly in this area. Agen is known as the prune centre of France. In the Lot it's wine – *vin de Cahors,* the deep-coloured, intensely ripe and gamey wines.

The Lot et Garonne is a land of discovery and adventure, a holiday makers' paradise.

On an historic note, one notices an interesting feature which occurs throughout the three departments; the number of town names which end in the syllable 'ac'. I was fortunate to meet a delightful guide, on a trip centred in Limoges, who was able to explain this phenomenon. This ending is derived from the Latin 'acum', meaning belonging to. The name of a place, therefore, originates from the name of a person who owned the land or property. Such as:

Nerac and Lavardac, in the south west corner of the Lot-et-Garonne; Montignac de Lauzun and Ferrensac in the north west; Cauzac, in the south east; Bayssac, Savignac sur Leyze, Courbiac, Montagnac sur Lède and Lustrac in the north east corner. Moissac, Ferrussac, Bournac, Couloussac, Engarac, Brassac, St Pierre de Nazac, in the Tarn et Garonne. Touzac, Prayssac, Lustrac, Carnac Rouffiac, Courbenac, Sérignac in the Lot.

Their size and importance ranges anything from a hamlet, or small village to the size of *Moissac*, a large town on the river Tarn.

In 1982 the association *'Les Plus Beaux Villages de France'* was created in Collonges-la-Rouge in the department of Corrèze, to promote small communities. They must be rich in national heritage, have sites of historic interest and have particular, striking scenery. The villages must have no more than 2,000 inhabitants and their exceptional beauty can be either natural or man-made.

From Brittany to Provence, from the Pays-Basque to the Alsace, from Normandy to Roussillon there are one hundred and fifty-one of them, spread throughout the ninety-six departments of France. Eleven of them fall within the boundaries of the three departments featured in 'French Impressions', and two of them within the tiny circle on which I focus; Lauzerte in the Tarn et Garonne and Pujols in the Lot et Garonne. Not more than twenty kilometres outside the circle to the east, on the river Lot, is St Cirq Lapopie, yet another *Plus Beau Village* which I specifically mention because it is so well worth a visit.

Meeting people within this geographical circle, I have come to know so much about the land, the traditions and the way of life. Talking at length to those who are featured in this book, I have learned about their particular lives. They have told me their stories; some born here, some came here. These stories reveal that they love where they live and wouldn't change it for the world!

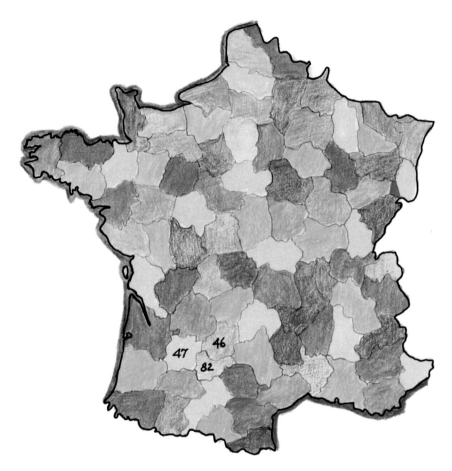

THE DEPARTMENTS OF FRANCE

showing the location of those featured in the book

46   LOT

47   LOT ET GARONNE

82   TARN ET GARONNE

Map drawn by John Taberner

Part 1

Lot et Garonne

'Le pays producteur de vacances'

Holiday Country

The Lot et Garonne is a country of plains, valleys and heath lands, limestone plateau and river banks. It claims to be the largest orchard in France. It's a department full of history, revealed to all who are interested in experiencing it through its ancient buildings, mediaeval villages, castles and numerous museums on a variety of themes. One can discover its beauty by river and canal, by marked footpaths, on horseback or mountain bike, or drive along the quiet roads. The department of the Lot et Garonne prides itself on being the land where holidays happen; its motto *'le pays producteur de vacances'*.

It's a department divided into six rural areas: Agenais, Albret, Marmandais, Guyenne, the Confluent and the Vallée du Lot.

Each one has its own particular charm and appeal; scenery, food, leisure pursuits, and tourist attractions.

~ *Agenais* ~

Agen, a two thousand year old town on the banks of the river Garonne, sits on the axis of the route between Bordeaux and Toulouse, it links the Mediterranean and the Atlantic, and it is the departmental capital.

In the Middle Ages it lay on the boundary between the tenure of the kings of France and of England. Famous names in history are linked with Agen; Eleanor of Aquitaine, Richard the Lionheart and Simon de Montfort.

As a university town it is proud of its academic forbears. One of the great French political philosophers of the Enlightenment, Baron de Montesquieu, though born into a noble and wealthy family in Bordeaux in 1689, spent his childhood in the Agen area, in the care of a poor family. In more recent times, the venerated Michel Serres, one of the most provocative of French philosophers, was born in Agen in 1930. As one of modern France's most gifted and original thinkers he is still lecturing at Stanford University.

Agen was elected in 1990 '*la ville la plus heureuse de France*' – the happiest town in France. 'How about coming to live here?' an invitation declares; 'for quality of life; the art of bringing together work and an agreeable personal way of life.'

It's a land of good food; farmers markets with produce of the season, fruits from the orchards and fresh vegetables, rubbing shoulders with duck, *tourtières*, speciality tarts of the area, wine and Armagnac. A veritable land of milk and honey!

Tourtières? You haven't tried them? Delicious, light, crisp filo-type pastry, folded like delicate butterfly wings above a base of apples, or sometimes plums, marinated in eau de vie. They are hand made, a real skill, and therefore a little pricey, but delectable!

Agen, world renowned for its prunes, claims the title of the prune capital of France. Of course the plums are grown throughout the south west but somehow Agen has claimed the prune as its own.

And its regional favourite sport? Rugby of course!

~ *Albret* ~

The main town of the Albret is Nérac where the navigable river Baïse divides – on one side is the castle and the new town, and on the other is Petit-Nerac. From Buzet-sur-Baïse you can hire a houseboat and leisurely ply up and down the river, playing at being an old fashioned bargeman. Take the opportunity of a wine tasting whilst at Buzet, visit the wine cellars, the *caves,* enjoy a wine tour with explanations of the vine and the wine. On the rivers Lot and the Garonne and the canals Canal de la Garonne and Canal du Midi, boating holidays offer you freedom to enjoy the unspoilt countryside and the local food. In days gone by, the old barges transported the renowned Armagnac brandy and flour from the Gascony hills to Bordeaux.

Of its history you can discover the old town of King Henry IV (famous for his love affairs!) who turned Nérac into a political centre, the town having become in 1527 the capital of Albret. Despite King Henry's philandering and his timely changes of religion, he brought through the Edict of Nantes political rights and some religious freedom for the Huguenots; restored to a degree financial order; built roads and canals; founded new industries and promoted agriculture. He is alleged to have said "There should be a chicken in every peasant's pot on a Sunday."

~ *Marmandais* ~

In 1182 Richard 'Coeur de Lion' gave Marmande a 'Charter of Customs' which gave to the town an individuality, a persona of its own, and economic development. The people of Marmande are today still proud of this Charter; their customs, combined with modern life, show the city as one with an eye to the future.

Marmande's rich historical past, its situation beside the Garonne river, and its protected rural environment, make this town, it is said, a pleasure to live in, both for its inhabitants and its visitors.

It has a wealth of festivities and celebrations amongst its varied calendar. There are flower and strawberry festivals, antique fairs, nocturnal markets and the International Grass Track. The town itself is of historical interest, parts of its 12th century city walls are still visible; a rose window in the church of Notre Dame; half-timbered houses of the XIVth century; and cloisters of the Renaissance period, not to mention the Saint-Benoit chapel known as the Bénedictines' convent, with its painted panelled ceiling. The four towers in the city represent the four doors of the surrounding walls of the Middle Ages. But the most symbolic door, the *Porte du Temps*, represents the city's passage through time and space into the third millennium.

~ *Guyenne* ~

North of the river is Guyenne, an important area for the production of animal foods. The river Dropt meanders through Guyenne on its way through the Entre-deux-Mers region until it reaches the river Garonne farther south. The River Dropt flows through the valley steeped in history where the Kings of France and England challenged and fought each other for over three hundred years. The result is a rich cultural heritage of mediaeval villages and *bastide* towns, as well as churches, abbeys and castles. The *bastides* towns of this period in history were the new towns of the Middle Ages. They were built at the wish of the feudal chiefs or sovereigns to attract inhabitants, to whom they guaranteed political, social and economic security. Each town was surrounded by ramparts on four sides with strategic gateways, the streets were laid down intersecting at right angles, the houses identical, with a market square which was the hub of town life. The shops were set around the square under the eaves of the buildings in the centre of the town.

Miramont de Guyenne, built on a plain in the 13th century, is an English *bastide* town now known for its beautiful gardens and flower filled streets. A Festival of Street Art is held here every year at the beginning of August, when famed international *troupes* entertain huge audiences.

These *bastides* towns are too numerous to name individually but a special mention must be made of Duras.

At the extreme western edge of Guyenne is *Le Chateau des Ducs de Duras*, of the Durfort family, built in 1308 by a nephew of Pope Clément V. It was at one time an imposing fortress. Gradually, since the 16th century, it has been converted into a residential dwelling. Its 35 restored rooms each reveal the style of a different era, with striking architecture throughout the chateau, such as vaulted archways and a secret room and a haunted hall!

From the top of the high castle tower the 360 degree view offers a panorama of the Valley of the Dropt, a grand view of the Duras vineyards and sometimes a spectacle of colourful hot air balloons.

In the basement of the tower is a museum of Popular Art and Tradition, Archeeology, Agriculture and of course Vines and Wine. Just near the chateau is *La maison du Vin,* where you can discover the wines of *Côtes de Duras;* red, dry and sweet white, and rosé wines.

Just opposite the chateau is the *Musée conservatoire du Parchemin et de l'Enluminure*. What a title! It is in fact a unique museum displaying and explaining the making of books in the Middle Ages; the process of making the parchment; the inks and colours, and the art of illumination. It is a small museum but fascinating.

In the central square of all these bastides, and in the tiny streets, you will find the ubiquitous markets with their local produce; a colourful array of fruits and vegetables, flowers and poultry, wine and conserves, and a mixture of aromas, amongst the friendly bustling of vendors and stall holders.

~ *Confluent* ~

This region, aptly named, where the two rivers, the Lot and the Garonne come together, is the heart of the department. The Garonne, described as an 'immutable grand river', arises in the foothills of the Pyrénées, it journeys towards the end of its mighty length, via Toulouse, towards Bordeaux and to the Gironde estuary. The Lot makes a 500 km journey, rising in the department of Lozère in Languedoc Roussillon region, it flows through five different departments, ending its course in the Lot et Garonne.

Agriculture is evident throughout this area, generating the main activities both on the hillsides and in the valley. Tourism is centred around the river port of Castelmoron and the various boating stops along the river.

On the banks of the Garonne, nestled in a loop of the river Lot, where the two rivers meet, is the small town of Nicole. Originally its name was Condé, or Condat, which simply means '*confluent*', or confluence. It sits under the *Pech de Berre*, a hill giving the village a protective natural edifice. It is a bastide town, founded in 1291 by the English, but was subsequently destroyed during the Hundred Year's war by the French, who then restored it two years later with the help of the protestant abbeys of Clairac. It was they who changed its name to Nicole. It was retaken by the English, attacked by the French again and destroyed all over again. It is yet another example of the presence of the English in this south west corner of France.

Clairac, ravished during the Hundred Year's war, was a protestant enclave. Many of its inhabitants fled the town during the war, to England, Switzerland and other northern countries. Sadly, all the former fortifications were raised when Louis XIII besieged the town in 1530. At one time renowned for its vineyards, it later became an ideal area for growing tobacco, where it is still grown. Along the streets, old houses remain where the coopers lived, making barrels which transported not only wine but also flour. It was the monks who contributed to the commercial development of the area, introducing tobacco and cultivating plums. Their Bénédictine abbey dating from 782 A.D, was restored and converted into an interesting museum called *Abbaye des Automates*, but unfortunately it recently closed. I had been keen to see this exhibition of models of monks going about their daily work, depicting their monastic life in the Middle Ages and I made the journey to Clairac - without checking up on opening hours! To my disappointment the museum had actually closed down. I only mention this as a word of warning, do check up to avoid disappointment like mine. Tourist Offices will give you all the latest information don't rely on word of mouth as I did.

~ *La Vallée du Lot* ~

Not to be confused with the Department of the Lot, the sixth and most eastern rural area of the department of the Lot et Garonne is known as *La Vallée du Lot*.

The principle town of this area is Villeneuve-sur-Lot, second in importance to the department's principal city of Agen. It was founded in 1264 by Alphonse de Poitiers, and as you will read later he also established the village of Monflanquin. His intention to rival the size and importance of Agen is evident in building a town over, what was for the era, a large surface area of 30 hectares. Villeneuve-sur-Lot has managed to retain some of its former charm even though it has lost much of its ramparts and fortifications. On first visiting the town you may think it has not much of interest to offer; not so, you have to look for it which will be easier with guide book in hand. Otherwise one needs to take a guided tour so as not to miss the history and culture of this town.

Villeneuve was, as it names tells you, a new town. Its fortifications were built by the community, though the gates were built by Edward I, King of England and of Aquitaine, as was the case at Monflanquin. Its towers were built a little later in 1313.

From its origin in the 13ᵗʰ century up until the 17ᵗʰ century, it was one of the most important ports on the river Lot. Due to its advantageous geographical position it became a major redistribution port, goods arriving and leaving from several different areas.

The boats, known as *gabarres*, loaded and unloaded their merchandise on the right bank of the river. For many years the boats were towed upstream by a team of men walking along the banks. Later boatmen rowed the boats which carried wood and cheese from Auvergne, copper and paper from Rouergue, corn, fruit and wine from Quercy, flour, prunes, brandy and cereals from Agenais.

In 1282, while the area was still dominated by the English king, Edward I, the original wooden bridge was replaced by a stone and brick construction. It had five arches, surmounted by three fortified square towers. These towers were part of the defensive system of the town, complete with portcullis and a projecting gallery, or parapet, with openings through which missiles could be dropped. It was in February 1600, over three hundred years after its construction that floods swept away two of the arches and the central tower. It was forty years later that Cardinal Richelieu ordered the construction of one sole arch in place of the two old ones. One can clearly see three arches and the large one which replaced the two which were swept away. Though called *Le Pont Vieux,* the old bridge, it also retains an older name; that of *Pont des Cieutat,* named after a mayor and his son who defended the town in 1585.

A fascinating legend lives on in connection with a tiny church at the end of Le Pont Vieux. It tells of three boats journeying along the river Lot towards the town of Villeneuve. Just before the old bridge they met a mysterious force and no matter how hard they rowed the boatmen could not pass under the bridge. Puzzled, one of the boatmen decided to investigate the waters and dived into the river to see if there were

some obstruction. Indeed he found a wooden statuette of Our Lady and with difficulty it was hauled into the boat. From that moment the boats were able to continue on their way. The story tells that the wooden statuette, which at some time had been placed in the middle of the bridge, fell into the river during the floods of 1600. It so happened that the boats were stopped just where the statuette had fallen into the water. After its rescue it was taken and placed in a nearby convent but to every one's amazement Our Lady 'escaped' and was found on the bridge on the spot from which she had first fallen into the water. Every time she was recovered and returned to the convent, she would disappear. Eventually the boatmen realised that she was demanding recognition and so a chapel in praise of her, was built at the end of the bridge and the statuette placed in the chapel.

It was as early as 1185 that the first barrage on the Lot was built at nearby Gajac, with a narrow passage at one end to aid navigation, a flour mill was built at the other end. The mill and dike belonged to the Abbé of Eysse, Pierre I, who was responsible for its construction. A toll was charged on all boats going through the port but during the Wars of Religion it was destroyed. In the 19th century the mill was restored and a commercial centre was built, accommodating a bakery, a saw mill and a workshop producing horn combs. In 1975 it was taken over by the French Electricity and Gas Boards but re-bought by the community in 1981 and is now a museum housing Fine Art and temporary art exhibitions. It also hosts other events. One such recent event was the *Salon de Livres*, a book fair where authors and publishers set out a display of their books, the authors ever ready to sign your purchase.

Throughout the town of Villeneuve you will come across a typical mediaeval architecture; *colombages*, the half timbered houses. They are of corbelled construction of cob and brick for the walls, with overhanging gabled galleries of wood. This construction gave extra living space for each house but not at the expense of restricting the natural light in the streets, already dark and narrow, nor of reducing the walkways below. At the upper levels of the houses, which were crowded together, these galleries gave the occupants the perfect outlook to watch what their neighbour was doing but at the same time denied everyone any privacy!

Most of the *colombages* dis-appeared during the 19th century, to the benefit of houses opposite them. The best place to see them is in the *Place La Fayette*, the social  and economic centre of the town. This square is bordered by covered galleries with archways underneath the overhang, lining each of the four sides of the square.

The name of the square was imposed by Guyot who left a legacy to the town in 1872 to build a fountain, which forms an attractive centre piece. The grand and ornate building is the *Place de Justice.*

Dating from the 14th century, a tower originally called the *Porte de Monflanquin*, was built about fifty years after the town was built. It was partially integrated into the fortifications, built of stone and thick Toulouse bricks. It symbolises the power of the municipality as six consuls, each the holder of a key, were authorised to open the town's archival coffer, sealed in a wall on the first floor of the tower. The third floor was the prison, where for example the baker was imprisoned for baking 'bad bread'! The fourth floor was a corridor around the tower for surveillance and defence. The Tour de Paris, as it is now known, is a reminder of the fact that Villeneuve was once an important stronghold.

The town was surrounded by walls on which were built six towers and gates of entry, of which there remain only this one – the *Tour de Paris,* and its twin, the *Tour de Pujols.*

The principal church, St Catherine's, reconstructed in a Romano-Byzantine style in the mid-1800s after the collapse of its vaulted roof, was built on the ruins of the former 13th century church, and is entirely in red brick, a local product. Though not an old building itself, the stained glass windows from the old church were preserved and incorporated in the new construction. Its tower is 55 metres high and can be seen from all around. If you take a trip to Pujols look down and let your eye follow the long straight road to Villeneuve and the *Porte de Pujols*, you can't mistake the distinctive red tower of St Catherine's rising above the town.

There's more to Villeneuve than history. If you are at all interested in horses, then a visit to *le haras* is a must. It too in fact has a history, when in 1806 this stud farm was created by direct Imperial Decree and is renowned for its thoroughbred Arab and English breed horses.

You mustn't miss the Saturday morning market in the main square, Place Lafayette. The stalls arranged around the central fountain are bustling with locals, which is indicative of the quality of the locally grown fruit and vegetables on offer. It is claimed that Villeneuve has the oldest organic market in France (other than Paris) selling fruit, vegetables and meat on a Wednesday morning. The bi-monthly Tuesday market fills the central islands of the high street, its stalls offering clothes, kitchen ware and gadgets, hair accessories, hats, shoes, and haberdashery.

During August there is a meeting of hot air balloon enthusiasts, *montgolfiades,* a colourful and exciting spectacle. There is also a Jazz Festival. Exhibitions, concerts, festivals, guided tours, fill the summer weeks.

And if you've had enough of history there are throughout the department many interesting museums for both children and adults; the prune museum at Granges-sur-Lot; the source of cork and the making of corks for bottles and jars at Mézin; nearby *La Forêt Magique,* the magic forest; a train museum; an exhibition of matchstick-made models of the Bénédictine Abbaye at Clairac, of Mont St Michel, and of Chartres cathedral. Visit *Le Chaudron Magique,* the Magic Cauldron, where children can mingle with the Angora goats and bottle feed the babies or milk the ewes, learn about the spinning and dying of the yarn and try weaving, whilst the grown ups can saunter through the shop and perhaps buy the soft angora knitting wool, colourful sweaters or fabric.

There are activity parks such as *Parc en Ciel* where, like Tarzan, you can climb through the trees with the aid of pulleys and rope bridges, but you need a head for heights. Theme parks, nature parks and gardens, a lily garden and *bambooseraie,* a garden dedicated to the growth of bamboo. There is something for everyone.

~ *Chateau-fort de Bonaguil* ~

A description of this south east corner of the department would not be complete without mention of the Chateau-fort de Bonaguil near Fumel. Its name *Bonne Aguille* means 'good needle'. On the very edge of the department, almost dipping its toes into the department of the Lot, it is thought that this Mediaeval fortified castle was built on the 13th century ruins of a keep, but essentially the castle as it stands was constructed between 1480 and 1520 by a powerful baron from the Midi de la France, Bérenger de Roquefeuil. Sitting on a rocky spur with difficult access, giving it its impregnability, it had a new system of defence based on artillery fire power, which in fact was never used! It is one of the finest examples of military architecture and is in an extremely good state with ongoing renovations adding to the enjoyment of inspecting its every corner.

Its position is somewhat set back from the main road, one wonders why it was built there. Apparently it was meant to defend the local border and the peoples of the surrounding countryside but it would seem that marauders or would be invaders were likely to pass it by. Perhaps that's why it has survived to reveal its towers and turrets in a reasonable state of preservation.

A week-long festival is held in the castle during August with guided tours, performances of plays, puppet shows, and a final spectacle of Shakespeare acted by students of a theatre group.

Chateau-fort de Bonaguil is much visited, and that's not surprising; it's a 'real' castle. It doesn't need too much imagination to visualize how it must have been in its heyday as you wander up and down stone staircases and in and out of halls and rooms. You can have a guided tour or wander around to your heart's content for as long as you like. I could say it's a great place to take the boys and dads for the day, but don't dare to leave the girls and mums behind, they will enjoy it just as much.

Places of Interest

~ *Monsempron Libos* ~

Do you love markets, ambling round the stalls, listening to the owners calling out their wares, choosing your fruit, soaking up the atmosphere and perhaps picking up a bargain? I do! Some people say that if you've seen one you've seen them all. That's not my experience. For me each one has its own mood and character but I do have my favourites.

It doesn't matter if it's fruit and vegetables, meat, clothes, household wares, leather goods, even mattresses! Yes, in France quite often you'll see bed mattresses for sale in the market but we have yet to witness anyone purchasing one! The atmosphere of a market can depend on its size and the place; they can be small and cosy, neat and orderly, higgledy piggledy or arranged in rows, or huge and noisy, but wherever they are and whatever is for sale, market shopping or even just browsing is fascinating.

Not far from the Chateau de Bonaguil is the town of Monsempron Libos with its well known Thursday morning market, a large sprawling affair, centred in the square with stalls stretching down along both sides of the main street. You can find almost anything here. Its competitive prices make it very popular with the locals and visitors alike and therefore usually busy, even out of season. At the height of the holiday season it's a bit of a crush but even that adds to the atmosphere.

Though I go to this market from time to time, my visits to the town of Montsempron Libos are usually on a Wednesday afternoon. It's half day closing and quiet. But I am going just a few metres down the *Rue de la Libération* which runs alongside the town square that is a designated car park when there is no market, and there you will see a shop window full of items made of hand painted silk; cushions, pictures, scarves, lamp shades, even ties. These items are for sale but principally this is where Madame Gilberte Larrive holds her weekly sessions teaching a group of ladies the skills of painting on silk. The lively and cheery Madame Larrive is 82 years old and has every intention of keeping her class going for years to come. I do hope so; I have made some very acceptable gifts here even though I am unable to attend every session. I have also made some friends who greet me each time I return after an absence with *'Ah, la petite anglaise'* which makes me smile as I am above average height. It's a warm welcome and I feel accepted. Then follows an afternoon of *entente cordiale* along with some hard concentration as we endeavour to put into practice Gilberte's teaching.

~ *Tournon d'Agenais* ~

At the eastern corner, bordering the department of the Lot, is Tournon d'Agenais, yet another of the stops on the Saint Jaques de Compostelle route.

Built in the 13th century on a rocky outcrop, you will climb quite a hill to reach the white stone ramparts. Walk through the arcades and into the square to see a strange moon dial. Inside you will discover the ramparts are in fact private half-timbered houses. Take your time, stroll around and make for the path which circles the village to see the astonishing vista from the view point, with a map set in the wall to indicate the towns and villages in the distance.

Every year Tournon d'Agenais has three fairs; the flower festival on the 1st of May and the rose festival at the end of August. In mid-August here's your chance to taste a *tourtière* at the *Foire*, the Tourtières Fair. In mid-afternoon there is a demonstration of the delicate and skilful making of the pastry for the tarts with a base of apple, pear or plum often flavoured with Armagnac. Then you will see why they are a little pricey but Tournon is where you must have at least a taste. At all of these you'll find all kinds of regional products on offer.

~ *Plus Beaux Villages de France in the Lot et Garonne*~

~*Pujols* ~

Pujols is perched 600 feet up on a rocky outcrop overlooking the valley of the river Lot. It has been inhabited since prehistoric times but it was the Romans who made the most significant impact on the village. The name Pujols comes from the Latin *podium*, meaning high place. The Romans secured the road from Agen to Périgueux and the crossing over the river Lot; from their high place they commanded a stretch of 25 miles along the Lot valley.

By the end of the 12th century Pujols became one of the most important strongholds in the Agen area when Raymond VI, the Count of Toulouse, took possession. By this time it had become a Cathar fortress soon to be ensnared in the Albigensian War when in 1208 Pope Innocent III declared Catharism a heresy. Cathars believed in the co-existence of two mutually opposed principles; one good and one evil, akin to God and Satan in conventional Christianity. Despite a crusade against Pujols, led by Simon de Montfort, the village survived the war. It was ironic that, then at peace, it was razed to the ground in 1229, when the Treaty of Paris left the people dispossessed and impoverished having to seek refuge in the valley of the Lot. Raymond VI's son, Raymond VII, who became Count of Toulouse on his father's death, conceded defeat to the King, Louis IX, in the war against the Cathars. He was forced to sign the Treaty of Paris which officially ended the war. Based on terms of the treaty, Raymond's daughter Joan was married to King Louis's brother, Alphonse. Alphonse de Poitiers, having mercy on the poor wandering villagers, ordered the town to be rebuilt, some distance below the old Pujols, the stones of which were appropriated to build the 'new town'- thus its name Villeneuve-sur-Lot.

At the end of the 14th century a large chateau was built at Pujols. Sadly there is little of it to see today; expensive repairs were necessary after the owners abandoned it in 1824, and in 1850 a misguided act of nothing short of vandalism by the local council sold off the stone to a demolition 'contractor' for a paltry sum. The stones were used to build a prison beside the river Lot at Eysses. The ramparts, already demolished in 1829 and the castle sold off, all that remains of what had been a fortress are a few stones and an illusion.

Pujols was, and still is, one of the major stops on the *Chemin de Compostelle.* Here, the sign at one of the gates of the village, declares the route number GR 652 and the distance the pilgrims have yet to travel, 1140 kilometres, to reach their destination.

What you see today of the mediaeval village of Pujols, is a sensitively restored town, accomplished during the last two to three decades. Pujols had flourished up to the 1789 Revolution but then during the next two centuries slowly declined. It is now in as near to an original state as is possible, with buildings carefully modified as art galleries, antique shops and restaurants. Pujols has refound its former status in its picturesque setting; it's no wonder it has been designated one of the 151 *Plus Beaux Villages de France.*

I never tire of visiting *Pujols* whether it's for a wander round the atmospheric streets, stopping for a coffee or ice cream at one of the restaurants or cafes, looking for that something special in the gift shop just inside the gate, or taking visitors and being happy to tell them something of its history.

My husband's favourite restaurant is here in Pujols, Lou Calel. Here they serve delicious classic and traditional dishes. One of my favourite starters is *foie gras* served on a pastry circle accompanied by melt-in-the-mouth caramelised apple. My husband's favourite desert which he no longer has to ask for, his wish is anticipated, is *Glace aux pruneaux à l'Armagnac.* Who would have thought that prune ice cream could be delicious? Try it. You'll find that it is. And mine; strawberry sabayon – fresh strawberries in a creamy sauce, with caramelised sugar on the top. The restaurant is run efficiently by smiling Natasha who anticipates your every need. You can sit at a table placed near the window, or on the terrace outside in the summer season, but wherever you are placed one has a magnificent view over the town of Villeneuve sur Lot below. As one looks down over the sprawling town it's difficult to believe that at the time Pujols was built, something over a thousand years ago, the town of Villeneuve-sur-Lot did not exist.

~ Monflanquin ~

It wasn't unintentional that we set out to see Monflanquin having heard of its charms, but it was by chance that we chose that particular day to visit. When we arrived the mediaeval festival – *Journées Mediévales*, was in full swing.

Walking the streets we were pressed on all sides by the villagers dressed in clothes of the times. Young girls in their long cotton skirts selling bunches of herbs, a grubby vagrant 'begging' on the side of the path, a child in tattered clothes dragging a reluctant dog, performers on stilts, the hot chestnut vendor calling for all he was worth to come and taste his delicious roasted chestnuts. Like magic, I was transported through time into the Middle Ages. In the central square an area was set out with games of the period. Then suddenly came the clattering of horses' hooves on the cobbled streets. Two splendid horses with their equally resplendent riders - handsome knights in their bright clothes, rode through the village. Displaying their coat of arms on their tabards, they carefully wove their way through the crowd. Underneath the overhang of an old building sat a monk, with quill in hand, teaching calligraphy to young children and adults alike. I had to try that. Round a corner in a narrow street a rope maker was encouraging a bystander to try his skill with the twisting mechanism, easier said than done! And how about learning to be a stonemason?

'Oh, how our children and grandchildren would love this!' we said to one another.

On that note we fled the village, raced back to our house and dashed into the garden, where we had left them having a quiet afternoon.

'You must come, it's just so exciting,' we exclaimed breathlessly. They didn't need much persuading and within minutes we were off again.

On our return to Monflanquin we had an anxious moment, not sure how our young grandchildren would react to two incredibly tall, terrifying witches with long tangled hair and black painted eyes parading round the square. They lurched through the streets on their stilts, cackling as they went. Accompanied by a smiling wizard, dressed in flowing black robes, we were reassured that they would not be casting a spell on us.

This *Journées Médiévales* festival takes place every year, usually in August and we never miss it. From year to year a different colourful theme runs through the festivities but throughout the holiday season

you are likely to meet somewhere *Janouille la Fripouille*. Janouille the Scoundrel is the town jester who walks the streets of Monflanquin telling jokes and giving guided tours. He begins by telling you that the village of Monflanquin was built 750 years ago, but it's all in French! Even if you don't speak French you will still learn a lot from just walking around with him looking, taking in the sights and sounds and savouring the aromas of fresh bread and pastries, hot chestnuts, sausages and always the ubiquitous pancake - *crêpes*, with lemon and sugar, or just jam!

This mediaeval village, bordering the departments of the Dordogne and the Lot, was founded in 1256 by Alphonse de Poitiers, the Count of Toulouse. Yes, the very same who founded Villeneuve-sur-Lot in 1264. It is recorded that Edward I, King of England and Duke of Aquitaine, rode through Monflanquin in 1284, during a journey through France. It is said he approved and endorsed agreements with regard to the fortifications of the village. These were built by the inhabitants of Monflanquin but the gates were to be built at the expense of the king.

During a period of 150 years, beginning in the 12th century, three hundred 'new towns' were built in the south west of France, one of which was Monflanquin.

As one of the 151 *Plus Beaux Villages de France*, it's certainly a place to meander through, discovering its treasures.

~ *Penne d'Agenais* ~

Penne d'Agenais, within ten minutes' drive of the town of Villeneuve, though not one of the *Plus Beaux villages de France* is within my special circle, and is certainly a village of charm.

The pilgrims following one of the *Chemins de Saint Jacques de Compostelle*, the St James' of Compostela routes, whether travelling from the north or west of France, would surely be pleased to rest in this picturesque village, perched on a steep hill above the river Lot. The  pilgrims still come here along with many tourists, attracted by its scenery, its history, its arts and crafts practised in the old part of the village. Their workshops nestle in amongst the old houses in the steep narrow streets.

There are beautiful watercolour paintings at the watercolour artist's studio; fine colourful fabrics, garments and accessories made by a weaver; colourful, polished stoneware pieces, decorative and practical, at the potter's; modern and traditional silver jewellery at the *bijouterie*; chic leather handbags and purses, belts and gifts at the  *maroquinerie;* fine tapestry cushions, handbags and wall hangings at the *tapissier;* sculptures, objets d'art, chased in tin, silver and copper foil from a metal worker.

It's difficult to choose and if you need time to ponder you can rest at the Café des Arts where Jean Paul and Carole Rouzoul will serve you. 'My name is spelt with a 'z'' he told me, and then with a grin, 'You know, like Mozart!' I already know how much he likes music and his choice, which ranges from classical to modern, drifts from the arches of the undercover café. Sit under a huge parasol on the terrace and choose a delicious salad, a coffee, a crêpe, a cool glass of cider or an ice cream and watch the world go by. This is another of our favourite places, we take all our visitors here. By the way Jean Paul speaks good English.

Perhaps you would like a more substantial meal, a dinner in fact in the evening. Visit La Maison sur la Place in the small square at the bottom of the old village. You enter this restaurant through an unpromising door straight off the pavement in the square. Once inside it opens up into a dining room, its decor all in white with a profusion of candles and unusual *objets d'art* which give it a Moroccan flavour. The cuisine often has a north African bent, with tasty dishes alongside typical French cookery. *Le Canard dans tous ses états* – in other words, duck cooked in many different ways, is always available. A favourite starter of ours is the *Salade mélange au Roquefort et noix* – crisp green salad with crumbled Roquefort cheese, scattered with walnuts and dressed with a vinaigrette. It's refreshing and tasty. I could go on but I'll leave you to discover for yourselves what other delectable dishes they prepare in this appealing restaurant.

In pleasant weather you can sit outside under great white parasols, in an extension of the dining room which looks into a large inner courtyard with a huge *trompe-l'oeil* on a facing wall. It's enchanting.

If you can manage to walk to the very top of the hill you will be rewarded by beautiful views across the valley, with the village of St Sylvestre below on the other side of the river Lot, a bustling little place on a Wednesday morning when the market is in full flow. At the west end of the village, high on the peak, is the church of Notre Dame de Peyragude. The word *'Peyragude'* derives from *pierre aigue,* meaning sharp stone. The dome of the church can be seen for

miles around and acts as a beacon, shining out at night when floodlit. Just behind the church lie a few remaining stones of what was a strongly fortified castle, built by the Duke of Guyenne, none other than Richard the Lionheart, who built several castles in the region of Aquitaine. There is not much left of it to see, nought but a few stones, but the very thought of this famous character having walked here, sets off the imagination. Young English visitors climbing over the grassy tussocks and stones can sometimes be heard and seen acting out remembered stories from their history lessons. At the opposite end of the village, still on the top of the peak, there are interesting old houses, and passing through the Porte de Ferracap there is an extensive view of the river valley.

Walking back down the hill again one passes through the only other remaining gateway out into the square. Penne d'Agenais has spread down the hill and though an attractive place it doesn't quite have the charm of its older parts.

We are fortunate that attractive places, such as Monflanquin, Pujols, Villeneuve-sur-Lot and Penne d'Agenais, are within easy reach of our home. Not just from the point of view of convenience have they become our favourites, but because they have so much to offer. We never tire of taking friends to visit them; they sometimes say to us, 'But it can't be very interesting for you going to places you have seen so many times.' On the contrary there is always something we haven't noticed before and we learn a little more each time.

The people you will read about now live within the section of the circle lying within this department but their work may often take them out and around into all three departments.

NOTE
For an explanation of the terms 'Cathar' and 'Albigensian' see page 178.

Christian Boncour

Osiérculteur et Vannier

Willow grower and basket maker

The weaving of baskets with osiers, more commonly known as willow in English, was a dying craft. Now the artistic skills of this craft are being revived by people like Christian Boncour. He is a real 'artisan', but this isn't how he first started his working life.

Leaving town life and a secure job, he and his family came to live in a 'chateau' in the village of Anthé. I would find it exciting to be able to say I lived in a chateau, in France, but Christian and his wife took it in their stride.

'It might not be an ancient building,' Christian recounts, 'but it is built of old stone with thick walls, built hard against the rocks here, which protect it from the north winds. It has been modified which means it doesn't look quite as grand as it did. But it's still a chateau.'

The previous owner of their home, a farmer, had at some time dismantled three of its towers, destroying some of its character at the same time. He needed the stone to build a barn and the *dépendances*, those functional and indispensable out-buildings, such as barns, that all farmers want. The same farmer also owned a second chateau across the valley. Both this and Christian's chateau were built around the early 1900s; one in the valley for summer use and one on the hillside, sheltered from the cold winter winds. The farmer had sold his summer castle some time before Christian bought the hilltop one, but the purchaser dismantled that too, stone by stone, and took them all away. No-one knows what he did with them – perhaps he built elsewhere.

Christian and his wife and family began a new life when they moved into their chateau. But how did they come to buy it?

'I was a fully qualified motor technician and mechanic working for Citroën in Strasbourg,' he begins. 'We lived in Theonville, where I was born, near the border with Luxembourg, not far away from the Citroën headquarters, but I was never at home. I was always on the road, Monday to Friday.' He shakes his head as he remembers.

'I had a good salary, my wife didn't need to go out to work, but it was not a good life for a family. We had two young children but I hardly saw them. They were growing up and I was not a part of it. All the responsibility fell on my wife and neither of us was happy.'

Christian interrupts his story as he tells me the 'children' are now 26 and 28 which highlights the time lapse since he left this life behind and became a highly skilled and creative basket weaver and learned to cultivate willow.

He goes back in time again and continues his story.

'I decided to give up everything, which meant a radical change to our lives. We wanted a real family life. We wanted the sun. We'd had holidays in the south in January and the winter, so we spent three weeks looking round three different areas in the south that interested us; the Languedoc, Les Landes and here – in the Lot et Garonne.'

'What about a job? Did that influence where you ultimately chose to live?'

'I'm afraid not. It may sound irresponsible but when we arrived here I didn't know what I was going to do, however I did have confidence that I could earn a living somehow. I was young and healthy and I loved the countryside and here in this area I thought about my childhood and the farming life, perhaps of going back to the land. You see my grandparents were farmers but they weren't sensitive to my wishes at the time and the farm was sold.'

'I liked the culture and way of life of working on the land, and that's how I began. I grew organic vegetables – onions, garlic, shallots, and I sold them at Villeneuve organic market. But I soon found that I had a lot of spare time and nothing to do with it. I needed to find an activity.'

It was at this time that Christian met the President of Villeneuve market who told him about basket making. Christian remembered the baskets that his grandparents had used on the farm and in no time the President interested him in the making of baskets and introduced him to the industry. Christian liked the idea, it was a creative occupation, working with nature, and so he did a little research into making a living.

Luck was on his side again when he met a *vannier*, a long established basket weaver, who was going to retire.

'Having had my interest awakened I was lucky to meet this *vannier*,' Christian says. 'I went to see him and I asked him an awful lot of questions.'

He was however, a little disappointed in the man's response; he tried to dissuade Christian from taking up the work. He told him that, since the arrival of plastics in the 50s, willow baskets no longer held charm and the same appeal. Nevertheless, he invited Christian to visit him and 'we'll see' he said.

Christian was not one to give up easily and he continued to visit him until eventually the *vannier* showed him how to make a small basket, but all the time discouraging him from taking it up.

'First, it was only a small basket. Then it was a large one, but always the same model - and not very exciting!' Christian says, trying not to be judgemental. What Christian wanted was to make progress.

Then came what he was waiting and hoping for. The *vannier* made him a proposition. He had decided he didn't want to retire completely, and perhaps the two of them could work together; he would teach Christian as they went along.

In due course Christian's teacher wanted his full retirement. He generously gave his machinery and tools to Christian but sold his *boutique.*

Christian had found a new occupation but he realised immediately that to earn his living as an *artisan* he must have some professional training.

'I heard of a School for basket making but I didn't want to go back to school with young people. In any case it was in the north and entailed a year of study. That would have meant travelling again and staying away from home. Then I discovered a cooperative near Tours in the department of the Loire, which I visited. There I met people of my own age – a new generation of basket makers!'

In Tours they were helpful, encouraging and understanding of Christian's position. They suggested that he could work with them, for the cooperative, from time to time.

'I went there for a week and learned to make one design for a basket. I made 50 of them! They paid me a set sum for each. It was great, I had earned some money! Everyone made the same model, but it was interesting to see that none were identical – each had their style or mark of the individual. For two years I did this, going back on a regular basis. Then I knew what I wanted to do next.'

What Christian wanted was to grow his own willow. As I sat and listened to Christian explaining how he went about it, I had nothing but admiration for his determination, hard work and patience. I understood why he needed patience when he told me that it's not until the third year of growth that a good harvest of willow is obtained.

'First I had to clear the ground beside a small lake. Willow likes humidity, it doesn't need to be in the water but does need to be near by.'

To become skilled at growing willow Christian followed a steep learning curve, discovering that there are 40 varieties - their development depending on the type of soil in which they are planted.

It was when Christian began to explain to me about the different types of osier, and having seen the beautiful objects that he had made, that I understood the significance of the different colours; white, yellow, green, brown, black and *rouge,* Christian described that as the colour of skin. He has six varieties which provide him with all the colours.
Christian no longer looks for an occupation to fill his time. Growing and working with willow is a full time job, and he is passionate about it. It starts in the winter when the willow is cut. It's then sorted into lengths and kept in water to make it supple. Then he can begin to work with it.

'What other kind of things do you make?' I ask him, having seen some of his beautiful baskets.

'Come and see,' is his response, and he takes me to his storage room. It is full of the most delightful, artistic objects, each with a useful purpose, as well as being a treasured article to own.

'How did you learn to make such beautiful artifacts?' I ask in amazement.

'It took time to learn, I admit. Teaching others is a good way of learning more for oneself. I took a job at Bordeaux teaching Travellers to give them a skill so that they could earn their own living. This was very good experience. Unfortunately it entailed staying in Bordeaux for a week at a time and again it wasn't very good for family life. I was offered the permanent position of Director of the Project to form a Cooperative but our children were studying and I couldn't contemplate going to live there permanently. Reluctantly I had to refuse the position.'

I work my way amongst the items in the crowded room; log carriers, a child's chair, a cradle, a large comfortable armchair and I want to sit in it. Baskets of course, to suit every purpose; linen baskets, racks and riddles, butter trays, florists' display baskets, containers for  strawberries, or oysters, in-and-out trays for the home office, and of course the attractive purpose made shopping baskets which are such a joy to use.

As well as working to fill this store room with such sought after handiwork, Christian runs training courses. In the autumn there are one-day classes for beginners and the more experienced alike. At other times, participants who wish to learn the craft may camp on his farmland, where there are full facilities for a pleasant stay.

'Some people like to go on holiday with the family, but at the same time want to try something new. Families are welcome here, adults and children, and if they don't want to camp there are hotels and *gîtes* nearby.'

Christian and his workshop are tucked away in the small village of Anthé and I wonder how people get to know where to buy his inspired wares and about his classes.

The answer is partly through open days at his workshop, when journalists come twice a year – 'Very good for publicity' he says happily.

'I also sell at different markets each week but I don't sell a great deal locally. Mainly I promote my business through exhibitions in Paris and I have good contacts in Strasbourg. I also sell my products in two boutiques in Paris and one in Angoulême.

Oh yes, I nearly forgot, one in San Francisco too!'

'So business is good,' I say.

'So much better than it used to be,' he nods. 'It's only in the last 5 years that people have begun to understand again the beauty and practical qualities of willow. Since the eighties people have been reluctant to spend money on 'mere' baskets; they didn't value the skill involved in producing attractive and useful artifacts.'

'No-one invested, like buying a painting for instance which would surely increase in value over the years, in such a thing as a beautifully crafted willow armchair or a cradle or even a simple but attractive log basket. However, attitudes have changed, fortunately for those people in France who began training round about that time and are now experienced willow weavers and workers today. Not only are these products appreciated for their use and decorative nature, they are also valued as a piece of artistic excellence.'

'It seems the south west of France was the right place for you to settle.'

'Yes, we found the things we were looking for; first the family life; a rewarding occupation for me; beautiful scenery and of course the sun! It took a while to become established but now we are very much part of the life here.'

'Such as your involvement in local jazz concerts. Tell me about that.'

'Yes, I organise a series of jazz concerts throughout the year, in Tournon d'Agenais. It's called Blues Station. I think we've become quite well known as a jazz and blues centre and we get some top professional performers.'

'I know your wife sings. Does she sing Blues?'

'Occasionally, but she prefers singing in a local choir. It's more her style, she says.'

Christian even has time to enjoy occasional mountain-bike riding – *vélo-tous-terrain*, or as the French call it in their happy practice of abbreviating names – the very popular VTT.

As I leave Christian, after our long and interesting talk, I can see that he is proud to be one of those *artisans*, imaginative and innovative in the craft of 'basket work', a term that in no way describes the dexterous skill he has acquired.

Nadine Migaszewski

Apicultrice

Bee Keeper

Nadine is a bee-keeper. She is a very modest young woman who thinks that what she does is quite ordinary.

'It's not a difficult, or complicated job,' she assures me, 'it's the bees who do the work.' But we would never taste that delicious honey without Nadine's complementary efforts.

Nadine is from a farming family who lived, and before retirement, worked in Moissac, where she was born. She has the growing of crops and rearing of animals in her blood and as a young girl her main job was to milk the cows and look after the sheep. Near their farm was a lavender grower who had beehives.

'My cousins and I used to run between the hives, weaving in and out, just for fun,' she tells me with an impish grin. Being in close proximity to the bees she became acquainted with their life-cycles and in honey-making. Little did she know that the childhood encounters with these fascinating and amazing winged creatures would provide her with a deep interest and give her a career.

It was after she married, when she came to live in the house called Passé, in Tournon d'Agenais, that she started her own hives.

'Your name is something of a puzzle Nadine,' I ventured. 'Migaszewski; it doesn't sound very French.'

'No, it's not. My husband's grandparents were born in Poland but came to France when they were young. His parents were then born in France, and of course so was he. But they haven't changed their name – they are proud of it!'

The mediaeval village of Tournon d'Agenais in the department of the Lot et Garonne, sits on a high plateau surrounded by the typical protective walls of the times. It is less than four kilometres from the border with the department of the Lot to its east and the department of the Tarn et Garonne to its south. Nadine's house is outside the village walls in the valley below and looking up one sees the ground rising almost straight up with the old village dominating the rooftops of the lower village.

'So, how did you become an *apicultrice*' - a lady beekeeper?' I ask her.

'I was eighteen when I took a four week training course in the area of Les Landes. I learned the rest as I went along, mostly by practical experience and a little reading. I've been lucky enough to have good advice from other skilled and competent beekeepers, which has been invaluable.' Nowadays, Nadine recounts with a rueful look, there are *schools* for learning the vocation!

She now has about 120 hives, some thirty of which are moved from time to time to different areas in search of acacia and chestnut trees.

The rest are fixed near surrounding villages such as Montaigu de Quercy, St Georges, Bourlens, Dausse, Saux and Anthé. These are moved, in what she laughingly calls the *transhumance* – 'You know, like cows being moved to different pastures on the mountain side!' But it all has to be official and a certificate obtained.

'I have to declare to the *DSV* (Directorate of Veterinary Services) every December, the number of hives I have, and where they are placed. They keep track of everything and issue me with an official card.'

The hives are populated with a local variety of bee, known as *le petit noir* – the little black one. 'Though it's possible,' she explains, 'to bring in a queen of another variety, I prefer to keep *le petit noir* as the core of my hives otherwise I find myself with hybrids, and the hive becomes weaker.' Her modesty shines through again as she says, 'I'm just an amateur on this subject and I prefer to make old fashioned honey.'

Nadine's work begins early in the year, in February, when she checks for the presence of 'varroa' in the hives, a reddish brown oval mite that is a parasite of honey bees. 'It's a real pest,' she tells me with a frown, 'and that has to be treated.'

In March she checks the body of the hive to make sure there are no other problems. 'We've had a problem recently with a hornet from China. It eats the bees!'

She grimaces in horror. 'They come into the country in packaging. I tell you it's an absolute curse.' Nadine is getting a bit wound-up about this.

'The only thing to do is destroy the nests but of course, we have to find them first.'

At the same time as all this is going on Nadine changes the frames of wax, ready for the bees to do their work.

'I don't push my bees – this is not a commercial enterprise,' she exclaims, 'I'm an *artisan*'. But she says this proudly.

In April she places the top 'story' on the hives.

'The bees need flowers, water and warmth. And then it's up to them,' she laughs again, 'It's as easy as that.'

The first flower to bloom is rape seed, and so her first harvesting of honey is in May from these flowers. This honey has an opaque, white marbled appearance, and is sweet without spoiling the flavour of whatever it accompanies.

'There's just one small problem with this first honey,' she tells me. 'If I'm not careful it crystallises with the first making. The later honey is the best.' Later in our discussion Nadine explains in more detail the question of crystallisation.

June follows with Acacia honey. A clear, pale greenish-yellow liquid. It has what Nadine describes as a 'neutral' flavour, very gentle; wonderful for adding to various foods. Delicious on hot goat's cheese toasts, pancakes and pastries!

'Toutes Fleurs', available from May to August, is my husband's favourite which we buy from her regularly in Montcuq market. It's a fragrant honey, varying in colour and texture depending on the flowers. It's delicious on bread or toast and equally scrumptious with *fromage blanc* – a soft white cheese somewhat like cottage cheese, often served as a dessert in cafés. Try it with pastries and as a luscious basting for duck.

The sunflowers bloom in July and August and from them the bees produce, not surprisingly, a yellow honey with a fine, smooth texture. Again it's good for use in cooking, and with cheese, walnuts, in cakes and pastries, and delicious dribbled on ice cream!

Honey from the chestnut blooms, in July, is dark brown and slow to crystallise. It has a deep, pungent taste and leaves a strong after-taste in the mouth. It's particularly good in herbal teas, hot milk and superb for making gingerbread. This honey has a lot of character and you either like it or you don't!

The 'Forest' honey is harvested from July to the end of August. With a fragrant but deep flavour, both on the tongue and in the throat, it's reminiscent of brambles. It is produced from *miellat* – sugar droplets which ooze from the trees' leaves and from other wood flowers, a phenomenon which occurs when there is a distinct difference in temperature between day and night; very warm days and cool nights.

Each honey has its charm – it's up to you to discover your favourite.

We come back to this question of crystallisation. When honey is first collected it is a runny liquid which in time will thicken and turn sugary. Rape seed honey can crystallise within eight days but most other types stay liquid for several months. 'It's a natural process,' she explains. 'The liquid honey you find in the shops, made by the large co-operatives, has been flash pasteurised. This stops the crystallisation – but it's not the same; it's not natural like mine.'

So where can we buy this yummy honey? I want to know.

'I sell my honey in the markets; at Montcuq on Sundays and Thursdays, Puy l'Eveque on Tuesdays, Luzech on Wednesdays, Pressac on Fridays. Then I've had enough!' she says with a grin. It's also for sale at the *boulangerie,* that's the bakery in Tournon d'Agenais and at the annual summer *Exposition d'artisans* in Montaigu de Quercy, an exhibition of craft work and foods held in the village hall – the Salle Ousteval – in Montaigu de Quercy.

By the way, when purchasing your honey, try Nadine's delicious cinnamon flavoured cake; of course one of its ingredients is honey. That's yummy too! Sorry you can't have her recipe, you'll have to buy some if you want to taste it! But here are some other suggestions for using honey in your cooking, including the *Petits gateaux à la cannelle* from Nadine.

Petits gateaux à la cannelle

Cinnamon Biscuits

Ingredients

110g butter

½ cup of sugar

1 egg, well beaten

1/3 of a cup of honey

2 cups of plain flour

¼ teaspoon of cinnamon

1 teaspoon of baking powder

Pinch of salt

Method

Cream the butter and sugar and add the beaten egg and the honey.

Sift the dry ingredients and fold into the creamed mixture.

Roll into small balls, place on a well-greased baking tray and flatten with a fork.

Bake at 180 ˚C for 10-15 minutes.

Makes about 30 to 40

Salad Dressing

Instead of the typical French *vinaigrette* dressing, try this delicious change.

(My alternative to avoid vinegar)

My husband doesn't like vinegar and this dressing uses lemon juice as an alternative.

Ingredients

½ cup of good olive oil

½ cup of lemon juice

½ cup of clear, pale honey

Pinch of paprika

½ teaspoon of salt

1 clove garlic, crushed

Method

Place all the ingredients in a jar, cover tightly and shake well before using.

Makes about 1½ cups of dressing.

This will keep in the fridge for several days.

Here is another dressing, more like a sauce, to coat lamb cutlets. It turns an ordinary dish into something a little bit more special. This recipe is enough to coat 4 lamb cutlets.

This recipe was passed on to me many years ago - its origin is lost to me!

Honeyed Lamb Cutlets

Ingredients
Grilled lamb cutlets to your taste.

1 level dessertspoon plain flour

Juice of ½ a lemon

1 dessertspoon of honey

150 ml of stock

Small gherkins to garnish

Method
Using the roux method to make the sauce, take a dessertspoonful of the fat from the grill pan and stir in the flour.

Cook over a low heat until brown, blend in the lemon juice, honey and stock.

Cook over a low heat for about 3 minutes stirring all the time.

Pour the sauce over the cutlets and garnish with sliced gherkins.

Honey Fingers

This is one of my old recipes which I used to make for my children. 24 of these didn't last long between three of them! It came out of a Women's Institute recipe book, compiled by members in a particular area, who remembered recipes their grandmothers' had given them. Where? I don't remember, it was long ago!

Ingredients
1 cup of rolled oats, fine oatmeal or Rice Krispies

1 teaspoon each of honey, cream, grated nuts.

A few dates, chopped.

Method
Mix all the ingredients together and spread on greaseproof paper to form an oblong about ¼ inch thick.

Chill well, then cut into finger-shaped lengths.

Delicious served with ice cream.

Makes about 24 fingers.

André and Veronique Coudert

Boucherie, Charcuterie de Compagne, Volailles,
Plats Cuisinés

~ *Specialités: Grattons du Pays – Pâtés et saucisses maison* ~

What a claim to '*Qualité et savoir faire*'! These are the very words featuring on André Coudert's wrapping paper and carrier bags – Quality and Know-how. But it's a valid claim. The quality of his meat and meat products is top class. He uses only '*Blonde Aquitaine*' beef - one of the best of the well known bovine races in France.

It was his dream as a young boy to have his own business as a butcher. He achieved it in the form of his roaming vehicle supplying the households of this district.

It was as a little boy, living in the department of the Charente, that André visited his uncle's abattoir, where his father was also employed. He watched his uncle at work and became fascinated by his skill.

'In those days,' André tells me, 'people killed their own beasts, hung the meat and cut it according to their own training and preferences, unlike today.'

Watching and learning from these early experiences, young André's dream grew. He wanted to be a butcher! However, even at this young age his ambition was taking shape with a difference. As he watched the mobile grocery shop travelling round the area where he lived, an idea began to form. What he wanted was a butcher's shop - on wheels!

First came the practical instruction and study. It was three years of learning butchery and charcuterie. Then André's boss sent him, as he did all his students, to a colleague in Paris.

'There you'll learn more about meat; the delicatessen trade, cold meats, cooked meats and last but not least the catering business,' he told him. It was a thorough training.

After four years André returned to the Charente to fulfil his duty in the Military Service, first at Montmarsan and then at the Military Base in Rochefort. Then he took a sidestep, those years of training proved worthwhile and he became a '*cuisinier*' - a cook! He now had two strings to his bow.

In 1980 André and Veronique were married and they began their working life divided between Charente in the holiday period - June to September, and from December to April in the mountains of the Haute Savoie.

'Both seasons were very busy but there was no work available in October and November you know, so we did temporary work - filling in for others on holiday, and maybe had a little break ourselves.'

It was a sad family event that brought an end to working '*les saisons*'; two different jobs in two different geographical areas. André's brother became very ill. They decided they had had enough of moving back and forth, so the young couple bought a house on the edge of the Dordogne in order to be near the family and André became head chef in a nearby hospital.

It was renting a house for short breaks that brought the family to the area of *Lot et Garonne*. Little did they know, on these weekends away, that one day they would live here. But the chance came when André heard of a butcher who was ready to retire and wished to sell his business. Here was the opportunity for him to achieve his childhood dream. The butcher's shop was sold but the roaming delivery van became André's. For eight months the retired butcher worked alongside André to acquaint him with all the villages on his route.

'He was a charming man,' André recalls, 'and helped me so much.'

Now there is a smart, new refrigerated *camion* equipped with all the facilities you would expect to find in a butcher's shop in the High Street. It gleams, displaying on the counter, under protective glass shelving, his top quality meat and charcuterie. All the tempting patés, sausages and *saucissons* are made at his home, with help from Veronique, André's wife, in their specially designed preparation room with cold storage. The stainless steel  equipment sparkles as you enter the cool atmosphere. The sausage mixing process is done by hand, or perhaps I should say by arm! Up to his elbow André churns the meat to mix it well. It needs strong muscles!

'That must be tiring and time consuming,' I remark. 'Couldn't you do it by machine?'

André looks at me a little scornfully. 'All mixing is done by hand – we are *artisans*!' he says categorically. I'm afraid I might have insulted him but he smiles comfortingly, that thick arm unceasingly churning the minced pork.

André's working day can begin at about three thirty in the morning (depending on the season) when he de-bones and generally prepares the meat to fill the mobile shop ready for the rounds. Then it's off to the markets, travelling from one village to another, back and forth across the boundaries of the three departments, as he supplies the local residents with their daily needs of fresh meat.

André is the epitome of a healthy butcher, with his expansive girth and rosy cheeks, his cheerfulness and courteous manner make it a pleasure to buy at his special roving shop. He now sports a small black beard, resembling a French impressionist painter, making him a very distinguished looking butcher!

During the holidays their daughter Laetitia accompanies her father. She is studying at Bordeaux University to be a veterinary doctor. Her studies are well advanced and after recent successes in her examinations she hopes to qualify in 2010 – yes it's a very long training in France! Her father is obviously proud of her and teases;

'Of course she will do well. Look at all the training she has had with me!' Laetitia works quietly beside her father, wrapping the products and dealing with the money, listening to his banter and smiling at the jokes she must hear time and again. André knows so many of his customers by name which demonstrates two things; one that they are regulars and two that he understands how important it is to make people feel valued.

'*Merci Madame, je vous souhaite un bon weekend!*' time and again he wishes each customer a nice weekend. André doesn't handle the money; with an extrovert wave he hands you over to his daughter, '*Je vous passe à ma fille Laetitia,*' he says proudly. He's a showman but he knows his 'lines' and he certainly knows all about meat – and how to cook it!

His clientele has grown and André had to have an assistant. Jaques who worked part time with another butcher, helped André on Friday evenings to de-bone the meat and then serve alongside him at the market on Saturday mornings. Jaques has moved on and now André, still busy, has another trained helper.

Each market day is different. Saturday morning it's Montaigu de Quercy, Sunday it's Rocquecor, Tuesday it's Tournon d'Agenais, Wednesday it's Bourg de Visa, Thursday it's Laroque Timbault in the morning, returning to refill the camion and then south into the region of the Gers until eight o'clock in the evening. Friday it's the rounds in the department of the Lot; Fumel and other villages. This is not to mention so many other stopping places in between those main markets, they are too numerous to list. He travels a minimum of 700 kilometres every week, and more in the summer.

'So that leaves Monday,' I say questioningly. 'A rest day?'

'No, no, no.' he exclaims. 'Paperwork; accounts, administration, ordering.'

Speaking of ordering I notice a board in his *laboratoire.* I'm in there watching him make sausages. Yards of them, or perhaps I should say metres, which are made at the end of the day, then hung in the cold storage unit, ready for the morrow. I read the list on the board out loud:

'Kangaroo, Ostrich, Turkey, Capon, Goose, Guinea fowl, Goat, Wild Boar' I'm amazed at the variety, and these are all alongside the usual cuts of beef, lamb and pork.

'Just for Christmas,' he laughs. 'Special orders for certain clients,' he nods with a wink.

I'm still watching the long continuous ropes of sausages, squirming onto the large metal platter. 'How many do you make?' I ask.

'About 300 kilos per week in the summer and 180 in the winter. On a Saturday morning I sell 70 kilos at Montaigu market alone. It's all those English buying for their barbecues!'

André also supplies the local school canteens every Friday, with the thinner sausages - like chipolata - again in long curling mounds. You don't find neat individual sausages here, you buy them by the yard! André holds up a section and you indicate how long a piece you want. That's where he breaks it into twisted neat ends.

After the rounds he returns home, some days as late as three o'clock when the van has to be emptied and cleaned. It's Veronique who cleans the van, taking about two hours to restore it to its sparkling newness again whilst André prepares meat for the next day. During the day Veronique has been busy in the *laboratoire* making beef, pork or lamb kebabs; deliciously meaty – no fat! Some evenings they do not finish work until eight o'clock. Bearing in mind their early rise the next morning they go to bed early. It sounds an exhausting life but both André and Veronique are cheerful, smiling people who love their work.

Finally I broach the subject of a holiday. Do they ever manage to get away?

'Yes, these days we do. We used to have only weekend breaks but over the last two years we have had a proper holiday. We go for three weeks to Brittany – and eat fish!' He laughs loudly rubbing his ample tummy. 'Makes a nice change,' he says.

It's time to leave. More sausages are still arriving on the platter – fat ones this time. But André stops for a moment and tears off a sheet of grease proof paper from a huge roll on the wall. He lifts a long string of the fat sausage and a smaller one of the thin sausage and deftly wraps them, folding the ends of the paper under to make a neat package.

'A present for you, for your dinner tonight,' he says, handing the package to me.

'Bon appetit!'

And I leave with a grin and profuse thanks.

This is not a recipe given to me by André but it seems appropriate to include it whilst on the subject of pork and sausages. Through reading different versions on the subject of the *cassoulet*, taking advice from French friends and neighbours and a little experimenting on my part, I have settled on the following recipe. But first a little history.

Cassoulet

A traditional casserole of south west France

The origins of the *cassoulet* are said to be from long ago – created during The Hundred Years' War when this south west area was ransacked by the English.

The poor people of the land were left with little to eat except beans and bits of sausage. Being resourceful they put these ingredients together and slow cooked them in a *cassole*; the word comes from the *occitan* language of the south west meaning an earthenware pot which gave its name to the dish.

As mentioned in the section on Tarn et Garonne there are many variations of the recipe. Acclaimed versions come from Toulouse, Carcassonne and Castelnaudary, which declares itself to be the 'capital of *cassoulet*'. Cooks both traditional and contemporary argue about the ingredients but the method of cooking is the same.

The essential ingredients are: white beans, that is *haricot blancs* – white haricot beans, pork, duck or goose *confit*, meat (mutton) and sausages. Some recipes also include slices of bread layered on top of the stew towards the end of the cooking, which turn brown and crusty. I prefer mine without the bread!

It's not easy to get hold of real duck *confit* in England but if you are on holiday in France buy a tin of ready prepared duck legs in the supermarket. The tins usually contain four to five pieces of duck; they are delicious and can be prepared in other ways too if you are not in the mood to spend time on a *cassoulet*.

If you are determined to make a *cassoulet* then buy whole duck legs, many a butcher will get them for you. You can precook them if you wish, otherwise just place them in the pot according to the recipe below.

Ingredients

500g/1lb 2oz home-salted belly pork

65g/ 2½oz duck or goose fat – if you have bought the can of *confit* from the supermarket you will have plenty of duck fat from the tin. It's economical and very tasty.

1 head garlic, broken into cloves, peeled and sliced – some of these will be reserved for putting on the slices of bread if used.

2 large onions, chopped

1kg/2¼lbs dried *haricots blancs* beans, soaked overnight

Large *bouquet garni* made from leek, celery, thyme sprigs, bay leaves and parsley stalks, or purchased ready made

6 good quality Toulouse sausages – or if you use English sausage choose pork with a strong flavour and with herbs

4 legs duck *confit*, cut into two at the joint

Method

Start by soaking the beans overnight.

Cut the piece of belly pork lengthways into three thick slices, then cut each piece across into two.

Preheat the oven to 180°C/350°F/Gas 5

Heat 50g/1¾oz of the duck fat in a six-litre flameproof casserole dish.

Add the garlic and onion and fry gently until soft but not browned.

Add the pre-soaked beans and the pieces of salted belly pork, cover with 1¾litres/3pints water and push in the *bouquet garni*.

Bring to the boil, skimming off any scum as it rises to the surface, then cover, transfer to the oven and bake for one and a half hours or until the beans are just tender (test as this can vary).

Heat the remaining duck fat in a frying pan and brown the sausages all over.

Lift them onto a board and slice each one sharply on the diagonal into three pieces.

Remove the *cassoulet* from the oven and increase the oven temperature to 220°C/425°F/Gas 7.

Add the sausages and the pieces of duck confit to the casserole and push them down well into the beans.

Return the casserole to the oven and bake uncovered for a further 45 minutes to one hour, or until the liquid has reduced and the *cassoulet* is covered in a dark golden crust.

At this point you may layer the top of the stew with sliced day-old bread, spread with crushed garlic. Put the casserole back in the oven – without a lid – and leave until the bread turns golden.

Serve straight from the pot at the table.

BON APPETIT!

Annie Novotney

~ *Producer of foie gras* ~

Madame Novotney is eighty six years old and talks to me quickly, almost too quickly, in her strong regional accent, so that at times I find it difficult to follow what she is saying.

What concentrates my mind is something I do understand, which she says within her first few sentences. 'Nobody does it for you!' This is her motto in life she tells me.

What she means by this becomes clear as she recounts some of the problems she has had to face in what she describes as 'not an easy life'. Straight away, Annie's strength of character, despite her advanced years, is still evident.

'I've always been independent, you see, I believe one has to sort things out for oneself, one has to be self sufficient.'

Her daughter-in-law is sitting with us and from time to time she helps me with some regional vocabulary that I obviously haven't understood.

Annie Novotney was born here in the house known as La Grèze, in the village of Saint Georges, and has lived here on this farm, all her life. Now, her son Jacques and daughter-in-law Raymonde, raise ducks and geese. Annie says she keeps an eye on things and likes to think that she still has a hand in the production of the foie gras and other products that they make.

Annie is proud of this land where she lives. She loses no time in telling me,

'You know, don't you, that the Lot et Garonne is *le jardin de la France*?' She says this with pride and she truly believes that it is the 'garden of France' and that there is nowhere on earth she would rather be. I wonder how much of the 'world' she has seen, or even of France? But later, I learn, when she talks about her husband, that she has indeed travelled.

Over the decades the farm has evolved from crops and animals to its present day duck and goose farm. Annie's childhood memories are strong and she begins to tell me in detail of the times when she worked on the farm alongside her mother.

'Oh, it was hard manual work in those days,' she sighs. 'It was so tiring, but at the same time it was invigorating and satisfying,' she adds smiling. I nod in what I hope is an appreciative way.

'We didn't have all that paperwork like today. There wasn't time for it anyway. Now there's too much of it. Forms for this and forms for that!'

Raymonde looks on and with a smile crinkling her eyes says,

'Everything has to be recorded Mother, for tax purposes.'

'Bah, tax!' she responds. 'There's too much of that too.' And we all laugh and nod vigorously in agreement.

After her little outburst Annie goes back to the past.

'I used to milk the cows, as a little girl,' she says, becoming quite animated again as she recollects her activities. 'I carried in the logs for the fire,' and she points to a huge stone fireplace in this vast day room. It seems to be an all purpose room, with an old oak dining table, much worn, at which we are sitting. There are two armchairs, one at each side of the hearth. The fireplace with its impressive two metre high mantelpiece, would take enormous logs. In a room this size, with no central heating in days long ago, it would need a vast amount of wood to ward off the chills of winter, and probably still does. At one end of the room is a heavy pottery sink, with a large old fashioned tap. It would seem that this room has seen little modernisation. Later Annie tells me there are bedrooms in a converted roof area.

'Do you know,' Annie begins again, placing her careworn but gentle hand on my arm, 'there used to be banana trees around this house?' I am incredulous and Annie smiles at my expression. Then she says with a twinkle in her eye,

'But there were never any bananas! It's not hot enough, you know,' and she laughs out loud. Then she grows serious and points to the fireplace again.

'I remember clearly the death of my father. I was five years old.' She pauses and stares into the black void, no logs or flames there now in the middle of summer.

'It was terrible, he fell, just here, into the fire.' Again there is a pause and neither I nor Raymonde speak. 'He never recovered.' She turns back to us with a wan smile.

'So you see my mother and I had to manage. We had to work the farm with just a few hands. There weren't many able-bodied young men around then you know.' She shakes her head. 'So many of them were killed in the 1914-18 war.'

I begin to understand her motto in life.

'Tell me about your name,' I ask trying to turn her thoughts away from those years of hardship. 'I've met one or two people in this area who have unusual names. Where does it come from?'

Ironically, my question plunges us back into talking about war – the Second World War. Annie was still a young woman when the war broke out in 1939 but now she is remembering happy days when she fell in love.

'I was twenty-three years old when I met my husband-to-be and he was twenty-five. He was an inventor in the Czechoslovakian Army, he was very clever.' She lifts her chin and says this with pride. 'He visited Chartres and after that came to the Lot et Garonne. But then the war broke out and he couldn't return to his homeland.

Eventually he found work in a factory, but it was difficult for him. First of all he wasn't French and consequently he didn't have any papers or a passport.'

'How did you meet him?' I prompt her.

'Ah, that was my brother's doing. He worked in the factory too and he felt sorry for the stranger, as he called him. "I'm going to bring him home for a good meal," he told us.'

In true story-book style it was love at first sight. They married from this very house in which we three are all now sitting. Their children were born here, and it is here on the same land that their eldest son Jacques, and his wife Raymonde, run their duck and goose farm.

It all sounded unbelievably romantic but far from it, as Annie relates. It didn't all happen without struggles and the same vexing question of no papers came up again and again.

'Hard times. War again, you see. So we had to be self-sufficient; truly independent. We really did have to sort things out for ourselves.' I'm listening intently to her and trying to understand what it was like. Though I remember the war, she knows that I am too young to have experienced the kind of trials and tribulations she went through.

'It was very hard for my husband but he seemed to have the same philosophy of life as I had. Even so, he had to find his own solutions and fortunately he did. A new life began for him, as a farmer and as my husband. And for me too, of course!'

Annie tells me how gradually conditions improved and eventually she and her husband were able to travel to Czechoslovakia. Even so it was a risky business. The 'papers' again became an issue. At a particular check point Annie was allowed through but the officials detained her husband. There was much wrangling and Annie proclaimed;

'If he doesn't go, then I'm not going!' It sounds like the Annie I am getting to know. But it worked and at last they were on their way. Later they were able to travel more freely to her husband's homeland.

Over the years the farm has changed. Now they raise different types of duck; Barbary duck, Tête Rouge and a wild duck known as Colvert.

It's at this stage that Annie takes me on a tour of the farm. First we see the Colverts in a field by themselves. I ask what must seem like a naive question.

'Why don't they fly away?'

'Ah, we prevent them doing that by carefully clipping a part of the wing.' I think I am frowning at the thought of such a practice and she quickly assures me, 'It doesn't harm them at all.'

The present day thriving business of raising and feeding the ducks and geese is still hard work but the fattening up of the birds is done by electrically powered equipment, supplying the food through a funnel secured within the bird's beak. And no, it doesn't look cruel. I saw the birds, quite happy to be handled and linked up to their food supply. They couldn't wait to gobble it up!

The making of the duck and goose foods is a time consuming task, meticulously carried out in the equipped dedicated building. The range of products is wide. Fine quality *Foie gras* - the salted and peppered, smooth, rich and traditionally cooked liver; *Confits* – meat cooked and preserved in its own fat; *Magret* – duck or goose breast for pan-frying, roasting or braising; *rillettes* – very tender seasoned meat, potted as a type of soft spreadable paté; and a selection of delicious pre-cooked dishes.

All these nourishing, flavoursome foods are bottled or packed in their spotless, gleaming preparation rooms. Annie takes me to inspect them and proudly explains to me the making of each product, showing me in sequence the use of each piece of equipment.

'I still help out, you know,' she tells me. And it's here in one of the store rooms that I take a photograph of her holding a jar of preserved duck leg, in its own delicious juices and duck fat. By the way, duck fat is beneficial to health – it generates the 'good' cholesterol in our blood, according to renowned specialists.

These products are taken to market and it was at St Sylvestre market on a particular Wednesday morning that I first met Raymonde. We talked about the *Confit de Canard* that I had just purchased and from that the interesting and pleasant meeting with Annie came about.

Monique and Patric

Le Savon de Marseille et Bijoux d'Ambre

~ *Quality Marseille Soap and Amber Jewellery* ~

I first met Monique and her husband, Patric, in the market square at Montaigu de Quercy. Montaigu Market on a Saturday morning, bustling with shoppers, is more than a source of good fresh vegetables, cheeses, excellent meat and local produce; it's also a gathering place to meet and make friends. That's how I made friends with Monique, bright and smiling, no matter what the weather, standing behind her stall on the one side of perfumed and colourful speciality soaps and on the other attractive amber jewellery.

It is thanks to Monique that I learned a surprising and exciting piece of history, right here on my doorstep. I shouldn't have been surprised by the existence of a 16th century tower, this south west area of France abounds in examples such as this; hidden treasures of the past, not intentionally kept secret, but unsung, as though people find such remarkable evidence of times gone by commonplace, and they have become immune to the historic value and significance to their present day culture. Of course, many such places *are* documented but often it's not until one meets a resident with an interest in history, that one is made aware of them.

Some years ago Monique delved into the history of two remarkable monuments which stand close by her home. She recorded her findings in a short historical document and I am indebted to her for allowing me to take information from her study, though she insisted that it wasn't necessary to credit her with the research, but that's typical of her kind and generous nature.

Nestling close to one another, beside the village of Hautefage la Tour, near the border between Lot et Garonne and Tarn et Garonne, is a magnificent hexagonal tower and the parish church, *l'Eglise Notre Dame*. Monique lives in the

village of Hautefage la Tour, her home right near the tower and the church. She couldn't help but become interested in them.

The 16th century Tour d'Hautefage was constructed during an era of high artistic endeavour and recalls the splendour of the past. The 15th and 16th centuries appear to have been a brilliant period in history for this region and both the tower and the church, thought to have its origins in a pagan sanctuary, were built at about this time.

Getting to know Monique and Patric took time. Monique and her husband run a stall several days a week selling Marseille hand soap and beautiful silver and amber jewellery. She appears at different markets all over the area, but on a Saturday she is at the market at Montaigu de Quercy. Our conversations were at first restricted to a few minutes at the stall in the market on a Saturday morning. We couldn't prolong our chatting and getting to know one another; there were other customers who wanted to buy the well-known soap from Marseille too and the fabulous brooches, earrings and bracelets!

Real Marseille soap is a natural product; it is scented using fine perfumes from Grasse, the famous perfume centre of France. Traditionally soap has been made in Marseille since the 18th century. In 1688, under King Louis XIV, the first regulations concerning the production and the brand naming of soap were introduced. These rules set by the Sun King are still in force today.

You will find it very hard to choose from the variety of perfumes, grouped into Medicinal, Plant Extracts, Flowers and Fruits, the soap bars glistening in their vibrant colours. There are the familiar perfumes; lavender, lemon, violet, vanilla, lily of the valley, wild strawberry, rose. Then there are the less familiar such as olive oil, eucalyptus, sandal wood, musk, patchouli, green apple and even lotus flower.

The same perfumes are to be found in small guest-soap size cubes. Each cube bears a letter of the alphabet and my granddaughters had much fun making up gifts for friends, by spelling out their names, cube by cube, all prettily wrapped.

Whatever you chose to buy, one bar or a selection, Monique and Patric wrap each bar individually in cellophane tied with raffia, to present as a gift or just to keep for yourself. My chest-of-drawers are full of sweet perfumed soap, scenting my clothes and deterring the moths! Try keeping it in a drawer for two or three months, it dries and hardens, then, when you come to use it, it lasts much longer! But this soap never loses its fragrance.

The amber jewellery comes in classic designs both traditional and modern in style. The amber is from the Baltic and all the pieces are set in silver. There's just one problem – every piece is so beautiful it's difficult to choose!

Running a stall in a market requires early morning departures Monique tells me.

'We get up about 5.30 to 5.45 a.m., depending on which market we're travelling to, in order to get there by 7.30 a.m. when they allocate a spot in the market place to each trader.'

'What's the farthest you travel?' I ask her. 'And where do you go?'

'About 65 kilometres.' No wonder she gets up early!

'I'm in Duras on Monday, Castillonnés on Tuesday, Condom on Wednesday, Monsempron Libos on Thursday. Then I work at home on Friday, doing my accounts and other chores. On Saturday we go to Montaigu de Quercy, and Sunday it's Roquecor. During the summer months, April to October that is, there is a market at Pujols on a Sunday, in which case our youngest son Damien runs the Roquecor stall – I can't be in two places at once and I go to Pujols.' Damien is a student, and though he wants to be a mechanical engineer, he hankers after having a market stall of his own.

'He loves the contact with people which comes with this job,' says Monique, 'but we've told him, after getting his degree he should work for a few years in the mechanical engineering industry to validate his qualification. In the meantime, during this summer, he has been working in the market to earn some money.'

'This is a full time job, isn't it? Early mornings and lots of travelling,' I remark.

'It is, but I wanted my own business. And so some while ago I started this.'

Monique goes on to tell me that she worked in the commercial world until she underwent serious back surgery.

'After my operation I retrained and worked as a secretary but the jobs were part time. Employers didn't want to take on a woman of fifty in a permanent position! That's when I decided to step out on my own and be self-employed.'

Years before, in 1986, Monique and Patric went to East Germany for a holiday. Little did Monique know that this trip would help her to decide what to do when, twenty years later, she was looking for her own business.

'The Berlin wall still existed then,' she says 'but it's where I discovered a small gadget – a magnetic soap holder – which intrigued me. I bought some for my own home and soon found that all our friends who visited us wanted one.'

Twenty years on from that trip, Monique tried to find a manufacturer in Germany who produced the soap holders, with the intention of marketing this little known product in France.

'What does one need to go with the soap holder, well the soap of course!'

And that's how Monique set herself up in business, not just with any soap but the best known quality.

'Without a doubt that's soap from Marseille. I also sell eco-friendly soap made by a German friend of mine, in Monflanquin, in the Lot et Garonne, and I sell loofa, the natural vegetable sponge.'

Monique and Patric added the new section to their stall to display the beautiful amber jewellery that they began selling a year ago. Necklaces, ear rings, brooches, rings, of shining golden yellow, glowing bronze and even the more unusual speckled green amber, are displayed for you to try. All very tempting and a precious memento of a holiday.

During the winter weeks, particularly around Christmas, the markets where Monique has a stall go through a quiet period. This prompted her to think about the *Marchés de Noël*, the Christmas markets. The popular Christmas market near Metz, in the north east of France, was the answer. Not only would she and Patric be able to capture the

Christmas trade they would also be returning to familiar ground. Patric was born in Marange Silvange, near Metz, in the Lorraine. Monique was also born in the north, in Hazebrouck, near the Belgian border. When they first met, the young Patric had a stall selling sandwiches but soon qualified as an electromechanical engineer. It was mutual friends who introduced them to each other and it is to friends that they return when they travel north.

'We go to the north east for two reasons. We rent a little wooden cabin, decorated with lights and Christmas trimmings; these little chalets are allocated to traders, just like the stalls in the markets at home. The Christmas market is right there in the square in the middle of the town. The second reason is we are able to stay with our very dear and long term friends. We are working of course during the day, but we are also having a good time enjoying one another's company and reminiscing.'

'There are Christmas Markets in the south west near where we live, but not of the size and status of those in Lorraine and Alsace. The markets in Bordeaux or Toulouse, for example, are for only one day's duration. The rent for the allocation of a cabin is extremely high. It's also too far to go there and back in a day and staying overnight in rented accommodation would further add to our expenses.'

'I'm intrigued by how you came to live in the south west if both of you are originally northerners,' I ask.

'In 1984 and 1985, a year or two before we made our trip to Germany, the winter weather in the north east was very cold, it reached minus 20 degrees centigrade. I heard of a job in the commercial business in Aquitaine, which was about to become vacant. Going south to better weather appealed to us so I applied for it and no sooner said than done – I got the job and we moved to Trémons, a very small village in the Lot et Garonne.'

'More recently we moved to Hautefage. When I was young we lived all over France as my father was moved from contract to contract. He was a Site Manager working on the construction of motorways, bridges and nuclear processing plants. He was transferred to Bordeaux to work, fell in love with the countryside and bought a house in the area. He died in May of last year and we decided to move from Trémons into the house that he had bought all those years ago. It's very old and has walls 80 centimetres thick. It has been unoccupied for some time and needs a lot of restoration, so we are in turmoil at the moment, in the process of reorganising the rooms and rebuilding the attic bedrooms'

'It sounds to me as though you don't have much time for hobbies and interests.'

'Oh yes, I do the decorating and I do a lot of knitting. Patric enjoys painting and at present is working on a picture of La Tour d'Hautefage, the tower right near our house.'

'You have two other sons who work some distance away, don't you? What about them, do you see them often?'

'Oh they are far away, and have their own lives now. Sébastien is now 30 and after taking a degree became a nurse in a hospital in Paris. Jérome is a doctor in biological research at Clermont Ferrand. But we do have a sort of adopted son of 34, who lives at home. He isn't actually related to us at all, he was a friend of our eldest son's. Some years ago he had a car accident and I went to see him in hospital. He needed to convalesce and I invited him to stay with us. He is still with us, part of the family now along with our youngest son, Damien. He works as a mechanic at the concrete mixing plant.'

Again this is an example of Monique and Patric's nature; kind and generous.

Go to any of the markets she has mentioned, and she will be there, smiling, trying to speak a few words of English.

'One of these days I'll learn English,' she says merrily. But don't worry if your French is not so good, Monique speaks clearly and not too fast as she describes the different perfumes of the soap and helps you to choose. You'll find it difficult selecting only one or two - but go on, have several, they'll keep, and they make good presents to take back home to friends and family. Not to speak of a piece of amber!

Part 2

Tarn et Garonne

Pays de l'Aventure Douce

The land of gentle adventure

Pays de Serres

Les Atouts de sa Diversité

Turns up trumps when it comes to variety

Through this department flow two majestic rivers – the Tarn and the Garonne – hence its name. It boasts a mixture of contrasting sights and interests, a joy to see and experience. It is peaceful, calm and uncrowded; about 54 inhabitants per square kilometre – that's about half the national average – in an area of approximately 3,700 square kilometres.

You are welcomed to this department in a friendly manner, its people hoping you will enjoy learning their history; with a smile and welcoming flowers on the tables when invited in, they press a glass of wine into your hand. Wherever you go you are invited to discover their gastronomic delights, in particular the old traditional recipes.

Paradoxically, in the story of people within the circle, the rivers themselves, the Tarn and the Garonne, do not feature. It is only the north-west corner of the department which falls into this circle, meeting the other two boundaries of department numbers 46 and 47.

When I first began to get to know France as a young teenager, I didn't understand at first why all adjacent departments (the equivalent of counties in England) were not numbered in sequence as are the Lot, number 46 and the Lot et Garonne number 47. It seemed logical to me at the time. It took a little while before I realized they were numbered in alphabetical order, hence most departments beginning with 'A' being at the start of the alphabet are single digits; as the names passed through the alphabet so the number is greater, reaching ninety six in all. That solves the anomaly of 46 and 47 next to one another – both begin with 'L'!

It was in 1808 that Napoléon created the department of Tarn et Garonne from six bordering districts. Its coat of arms took the symbols from four of the areas concerned; Rouergue, Gascony, Languedoc and Guyenne.

Montauban is the capital of this department situated on the River Tarn. It is a *bastide* town, one of the first new towns to be built according to the Foundation Charter.

During the Middle Ages the drawing up and signing of a Foundation Charter was necessary before any building work could begin. There were strict rules with regard to the symmetrical layout and the building of a covered market place or hall. The Charter also set out the rights and responsibilities of the inhabitants of the new town.

These former fortified towns and villages, known as *bastides*, which are common in this part of France, are some of the earliest examples of town planning in the south west of the country.

Montauban is generally seen as the oldest of the *bastide* towns in the south of France, after Mont-de-Marsan. Founded in 1144 by Alphonse Jourdain, count of Toulouse, as a defence against both the English and the French Royal might, it has endured a volatile history. Like so many of the towns in the south west of France it suffered in the Albigensian war, a religious war to eliminate the heretical beliefs of the Albigensian sect, and in 1360 was ceded to the English though they were driven out by the inhabitants in 1414. It was 150 years later that the bishops of the area adopted Protestantism and thus *Montauban* became one of the four Huguenot strongholds under the Peace of Saint-Germain. Alas, this peace was unstable. Several factors, including the irregular marriage between the Catholic daughter of Catherine de Medici to the Protestant Prince Henry of Navarre, without the Pope's permission, incited in 1572 the already anti-Huguenot Parisians into mob violence and this rioting spread through France. Thousands and thousands of Huguenots died, not only in Montauban, but in several major towns – Toulouse, Bordeaux, Lyon, Bourges, Rouen, and Orléans.

Prince Henry of Navarre became King Henry IV of France in 1589 and it was he who in 1598, granted Protestants (generally Huguenots in France), through the Edict of Nantes, the liberty of private and public worship along with full civil rights. The Catholic Louis XIV crowned king in 1654 at the age of 15, came to believe that there should be religious unity in France and initially urged his Protestant subjects to convert to 'the King's religion', even though he bore them no ill will. However his Roman Catholic advisers persuaded him to repeal the Edict and in 1685 the Protestants again endured persecution.

Montauban enjoyed prosperous times in between the wars and by the time of the Revolution it had once more become a rich city, as a consequence of its success in the manufacture of cloth.

In the centre of the town is *La Place Nationale.* You enter this pleasant red-brick square by one of four porticos. The shops are sheltered by a double row of arcades. The graceful 17th century facades are seen to advantage from the centre, where you can then appreciate the sun dial.

The history of Montauban is very much in evidence in the 13th century Eglise Saint Jacques and La Cathédrale Notre Dame.

The *Eglise,* dedicated to Saint James of Compostela, was funded from heavy taxes demanded of the rich, but suffered as did so many buildings in the south west from the several wars and religious unrest. It was during the Wars of Religion that the Calvinists (who were Protestants) knocked down the vault and the spire of the church. On the octagonal bell tower there is evidence of damage from cannon balls from Louis XIII siege in 1621. A speciality of Montauban is *Boulets de Montauban,* Montauban cannon balls which are in fact hazelnuts coated in chocolate, created to commemorate the Huguenots' defiance.

It was Cardinal Richelieu who restored some religious peace and ordered the reconstruction of the church. Along both sides of the south nave, which is in French gothic style, are three chapels. The painting in the second chapel on the right is by Joseph Ingre, father of the famous painter Jean-August-Dominique Ingres, and is dedicated to Saint Jacques, the patron saint of the church.

On the site of the one time residence of the bishops of Montauban, and later a castle of the Counts of Toulouse, is the Musée Ingres. Known as Jean Ingres, this famous artist was born in Montauban and his birth is commemorated by an ornate monument. It houses the largest collection of paintings by Ingres in the world.

La Cathédrale Notre Dame houses a famous work by Jean Ingres, the 'Vow of Louis XIII'. Other than that, its claim to fame is that it marks the triumph of the Catholic religion over this Protestant town, after the repeal of the Edict of Nantes.

The old bridge over the river Tarn, *Le Pont Vieux*, was ordered by Philippe Le Bel in 1304. Its construction, taking almost thirty years to complete, made it the best crossing-point on the Tarn for miles around. The bridge's flat road, a rare feature in the Middle Ages, is 205 metres long. Its seven pointed arches each with a beak-like spout allowed water to escape in times of flood. Once upon a time there was a square tower at each end of the bridge as part of the town's defences. The one on the right bank housed the torturer! but it was destroyed in 1663 in order to build *Le Palais Episcopal.* The second tower, demolished in 1701, was replaced with a triumphal arch to celebrate a victory of Louis XIV. Similar to the bridge at *Avignon,* a small chapel, dedicated to *Sainte Catherine* the patron saint of boatmen, was built over the fourth support.

Montauban is a *ville fleurie,* with beautiful and well cared for gardens adorning the town. The oldest is *Le jardin de l'Evêque;* the bishop of Montauban designed the garden in 1674. Flower beds, an arbour and an orangery formed a magnificent part of his design, but sadly these faded away after the Revolution.

Today you can enjoy a three hectares arboretum, created in 1860, on the steep slopes of the Tescou stream which crosses the area. Cedars, Virginian Tulip trees and ginko-bilobas flourish here.

In 1679 the *Cours Foucault*, a tree-lined esplanade overhanging the river Tarn was established in 1679 by Nicolas Foucault, and has served over the years as a centre for military revues, the regular agricultural show and various other events.

More recently, in 1972, a rose garden of over a thousand varieties, mostly non-native or rare species, was established by Roger Sucret. In 1996 it was renamed *Espace François Mitterand* and after several gifts now comprises over 16,000 plants.

Montauban is today linked again to the sea through the canal, re-opened after extensive work, affording those who love 'messing about in boats' the opportunity of a delightful holiday. Whether it be a house-boat, barge or even a *bateau électrique*, a small electric powered boat, even a surf-bike, there is something for everyone. Regaining this link, lost some years ago, has also opened up leisure pursuits for fishermen, joggers and strollers along the old towpath.

Four kilometres from the point where the river Tarn flows into the river Garonne, lies Moissac. It is a modern town, mostly due to the rebuilding after damage it suffered in 1930 when the Tarn, swollen by a sudden thaw in the Massif Central, burst its banks and flooded the town. Over six hundred houses were destroyed and 120 people died. The *Canal Latéral* of the Garonne also passes through Moissac.

Believed to have been founded in the 7th century Moissac went through numerous wars like Montauban, and although there are some interesting parts in the old town, it is the Abbey church of St Pierre for which it is well known.

This Romanesque church was consecrated in 1063 and through the following century was enlarged. During this period the superb south porch was built, with its glorious carving depicting Christ, right hand in benediction and the Book of Life in his left. This fine work served as a model for other artists who decorated the porches of many churches across the south of France.

This Abbey survived not only the siege of Simon de Montfort in 1212, which is remarkable, but also its use during the Revolution as a gunpowder factory and billet for soldiers. The soldiers left their mark, sadly, by damaging many of the sculptures.

On the north side of the church is the Cloister surrounding a garden; these are the oldest Cloisters in the whole of France significant for their rich carvings and symmetry. A splendid cedar tree offers shade in this tranquil place. Seventy six marble columns supported the pantile roof of the cloister; each column bears an inverted wedge-shaped stone skilfully and gracefully carved with animals, plants and scenes from the Bible. Look on the west side, on the middle pillar you will see an inscription telling that the Cloister was made in the Year of our Lord 1100.

Beside the abbey is a small museum of regional art and craft; paintings, drawings by local people and artefacts discovered in archaeological digs in the area. The museum also contains an interesting exhibition of furniture from across the region.

The magnificent and varied scenery of the Tarn et Garonne is a result of the differing geographical regions; north, north east, central and south west. Each offers the sightseer or holiday-maker something different.

In the north you are in the low foothills of the Massif Central, the slopes of Quercy. Here you find vineyards, orchards, woods and meadows, the dignified cypress trees a dominant feature.

The central area is a narrow plain with extensive orchards. Both rivers flow through this area, as does the *Canal Latéral*. The A20 running from the north, from Paris through Limoges, and the A62 running from the west through Agen, provide good communication links. This area is dominated by the historic cities of Montauban, the county town, Moissac and Valence d'Agen.

In the north east is the craggy Quercy plateau, its limestone soil providing ideal growing conditions for junipers and oaks. Dry stone walls edge the pathways, the dizzy heights of the land dropping into the spectacular gorges of the bordering department of Aveyron.

It is in the south west that the peaks of the Pyrenees come into view. The countryside here is undulating; cereals, sunflowers and garlic are grown on the Gascony slopes.

Holidaying in any of these regions, one cannot help but walk in the footsteps of the pilgrims of Saint James of Compostela.

Perhaps, before you read of the numerous stopping places on the pilgrimage trail, an explanation of the legend will help you understand the symbols found on buildings and at the entrances to many of the mediaeval villages on the different routes to Saint James' shrine at Compostela.

First of all, let's ask – who was Saint James?

James was the son of Zebedee and Marie-Salome. He was a contemporary of Jesus Christ and one of the first of his disciples along with his brother John, and Peter and Andrew; the four of them fishermen.

After Christ's death James, a tireless preacher full of ardour, went to preach the gospel in Andalucía in Spain. After several years he returned to Palestine and with the other Apostles, preached even in the synagogues. Herod became so annoyed with James' behaviour that he resolved to teach the Christian community a lesson; he had James beheaded in 44 AD; the first Apostle to be martyred.

The Apostles put James' body in a small craft which came ashore seven days later in Galicia. The tomb which had been erected to him was abandoned. It was not until the 9th century that the appearance of a star showed the place where James' body lay. This is where the church built by Alphonse II, King of Galicia, and the town of Santiago (which in English means 'Saint James') were to arise in about 820. The name Campus Stella, meaning 'field of the star', was added and linked to that of Saint James. Over time it became *Compostelle*. The church was subsequently destroyed by the Moors in 997 AD, but rebuilt in 1088 and became a sacred and important place and pilgrim centre. Over centuries it has developed and now, many years later, it is the destination of a significant and popular pilgrimage.

This pilgrimage trail is about 900 km long and has been walked for over 1,000 years. Another legend states that Saint James' remains were taken by his disciples to northern Spain and buried on the site, now known as *Santiago de Compostela*.

Stories of the discovery of the Apostle's tomb brought pilgrims from around Europe; and since the 9th century they have been visiting the shrine dedicated to Saint James. In the Middle Ages it was the most important of Christian pilgrimages.

Pilgrims were catered for in hostels on the way, with all the trappings of tourism. It is hard to believe that an extraordinary guide-book existed, the Codex Calixtinus put together in about 1140, along with the sale of souvenirs and badges. It sounds all too familiar.

A waning in the numbers making the long and arduous journey was a consequence of the Protestant Reformation, along with political unrest in the 16th century. It wasn't until the mid 20th century, when travelling became easier, people realised that making a pilgrimage was not beyond their pockets and they began to take up the route again.

Known in France as *Le Chemin de Saint Jacques*, this pilgrim route is now walked today by increasing numbers of people, since the late 1980s this includes a growing number of pilgrims from all over the world.

In 1987 the Council of Europe declared this route the first European Cultural Route, categorised as being of special European interest. In 1993 it was inscribed as one of UNESCO's World Heritage Sites.

There are four main pilgrimage routes in France ; their starting points are Paris via Tours, Vézelay, Le Puy and Arles, forming a network of particular historic and architectural interest, converging in the Basque country of the western Pyrenees. The pilgrim route GR 65 passes through Lauzerte, Moissac and Auvillar in the Tarn et Garonne. A notable stopping place is the Benedictine Abbey of Saint Pierre, in Moissac, which was described earlier.

The routes and stopping places, used for centuries, are visibly marked by the *coquille*, the scallop shell. Santiago de Compostela is in the province of Galicia, northern Spain, where scallop shells abound, thus the custom of carrying back a shell as proof of the journey led to it being adopted as a symbol of all pilgrims. There is a legend associated with the route of it being a fertility pilgrimage during pagan times. The shell is seen as protecting life, connected with the womb, birth and creation; thus it is reasoned as the origin of the scallop as a symbol of the pilgrimage.

The beggar's pouch and scallop shell are still carried by modern-day pilgrims. You may undertake the journey today but to fulfil the requirements of a true pilgrimage it must be made on foot, bicycle or on horseback. The pilgrim has a passport, which is stamped along the Way, has use of free hostels – which are known as the *Haltes sur les Chemins de Saint Jacques,* and has the passport certified at the Cathedral in Santiago. To do the whole route, travelling at about 30 km a day, it will take about thirty days. If all you want is to have your Certificate stamped at the Cathedral you must walk at least 100 km, or cycle 200 km. Your passport will be stamped at the free lodgings or shelters as you stop at each *Halte,* and serves as proof of the completion of the pilgrimage.

The following is typical of the kind of songs the pilgrims chanted to keep up their spirits as they tramped along.

Tous les matins nous prenons le Chemin,
Tous les matins nous allons plus loin,
Jour après jour la route nous appelle,
C'est la voix de Compostelle.

Every morning we set off on the road,
Every morning we go a little farther,
Day after day the route calls us.
It's the voice of Compostela.

~ *Les Plus Beaux Villages de France* ~

Three of Tarn et Garonne's villages carry the classification of 'Un des plus Beaux Villages de France': Bruniquel on the eastern border, Auvillar on the western edge and Lauzerte in the north west corner of the department. Only Lauzerte comes within the geographical circle in which the individuals described in this book live and work, you'll find its description in the section 'Within the Circle'.

To earn the categorization of '*Plus Beaux Villages*' the three villages had to go through a rigorous inspection and survey by the '*Association des Plus Beaux Villages de France*'. Auvillar, and its locality, known as the land of the troubadours and poets, is, like Lauzerte and Bruniquel, a stop on the *Chemin de Saint Jacques de Compostelle,* which in itself is an encouragement to visit or even make a detour if travelling in the area.

~ *Bruniquel* ~

Bruniquel is a fortified market town built high on a rocky promontory above the Aveyron river where it joins the river Vère. The town is on the very edge of the department of Tarn et Garonne and from its magnificent position it looks down into the neighbouring department of the Aveyron. It has an imposing fortress built in the 6th century and a chateau, built on foundations of the same period, which is open to visitors. Evidence of Bruniquel's prosperity during the Middle Ages, attributable to its location as a crossing point for merchants as well as being a stopping place for the pilgrims en route to Santiago de Compostela, can be seen in the decorated turrets, carved figures and sculptured stone doorways.

~ *Auvillar* ~

Auvillar is a fascinating village and though it does not fall within the circle, I can't help but tell you about it in detail, as it is worth seeing, especially as it is one of the *Plus Beaux Villages.*

My husband and I visited Auvillar one cold but bright day in early November. On arrival there was not a soul to be seen; the bar cum restaurant, outside which we had parked our car, looked dark and not even open for business. We had so looked forward to seeing what we had read about that we looked at each other in dismay, wondering if our journey at this time of year was to be a disappointment. The 'bar' was in fact open and a hot *grand crème,* and the promise of an appetising lunch, in what turned out to be a very pleasant restaurant, revived our spirits.

We entered the village, passing through the archway of the gate which is in fact the clock tower, and walked down the cobbled street leading us to the main square, *la Place de la Halle.* What a surprise to find

that it is not a square but is in fact a triangle. There in the middle is a circular construction with a tiled roof with a flag flying. It is built on Tuscan style columns and houses at its centre a small remarkably symmetrical, circular arcade. Built relatively recently, it is nevertheless interesting in its circular construction, with two types of grain measuring equipment inside. These metal measures date from the construction of the *Halle* in 1824, the others – cut into the stone – remain from the former rectangular building which was to be found earlier in the centre of the market place.

This pretty triangular area is bordered by 17th and 18th century half-timbered houses and in *la rue des Nobles* you'll see the half-timbered and corbelled houses of the Middle Ages.

As a Gallo-roman town, a victim of numerous invasions until the 10th century, in particular by the Normans, it became in the 11th century the chief town of a viscountcy. In the 14th and 15th centuries it was owned by the Counts of Armagnac; later it was the private kingdom of the Kings of Navarre until eventually in 1589, it was brought under the French crown with the accession of Henry IV, himself a King of Navarre. As a stronghold, its situation subjected it to all the conflicts which ravaged the area; the crusade against the Albigeois, the Hundred Years War and the various wars of religion.

From the 17th to the 19th centuries, Auvillar owed its prosperity to two industries; glazed earthenware and the making of goose quills for calligraphy, both taking advantage of its proximity to the river Garonne. By the 19th century traffic on the river had reached 3,000 barges each year.

La Musée d'art et traditions populaires has a very interesting collection of Auvillar pottery from the 18th and 19th centuries.

Despite the ravages of numerous attacks, some buildings of architectural interest survived, such as La Porte Arnaud Othon, named after one of the Counts of Auvillar. Known as the *Tour de l'horloge,* this clock tower, built over the arched gateway, was constructed in stone and rose brick during the reign of Louis XIV. It is topped by a mansard roof decorated with a wrought iron cage. The clock in the tower was added in the 19th century.

The Parish Church of St Peter is outside the village walls. It was successively demolished and rebuilt over the centuries, but was already in existence in 1186. It has an attractive rose window, mostly in bright blues, above the south door. Classed as an Historic Monument it is one of the most beautiful churches in the diocese of Montauban.

Having read of the underground fountain, the Roman drinking trough, wash house and ancient well, we set off along the narrow and cobbled streets, armed with a village street map to find the old Roman street *le Peyrat*. The fountain, underneath this street, fed the trough and wash house which you can still see from the road, though at first you might not recognise it! We had read that this area had been converted into an aquarium and to our amazement the trough of dark water was indeed full of trout, a sight not quite equal to the picture that had been conjured up in our minds!

Underground are the tunnels; photographs were taken when the tunnels were discovered, these show a series of galleries, rooms and drains, which, it turns out, pass under the whole village, one of the drains running beside the clock tower.

I have to say you could be disappointed by the fact that this underground network of tunnels cannot be visited, and the drinking trough and wash house are not very photogenic. Even so one stands in awe as one is reminded that these remains are Roman, well over a thousand years old, and still there!

At this point we met a villager walking her dog who greeted us cheerfully and we exchanged comments on our relative dogs. This gave me the opportunity to ask how to find Sainte Catherine's chapel. My curiosity is such that I wanted to see a 9th century stone monogram which is placed above the door of this tiny chapel.

Of course, it's locked, which meant a visit to the *Mairie* to find out if we could borrow the key. The Mayor was helpful

Monogramme du Christ de l'époque carolingienne (9e siècle), façade de l'église du port à Auvillar

and accompanied us to the chapel and there above the door was the stone monogram. 'I'm afraid it's rather worn away,' he said. I nodded, trying to look pleased when in fact I was disillusioned. Such was the description of this Carolingien monogram which I had read about in a brochure, that I felt it was something rare and exceptional. Had I not seen a clear picture of it I would not have been able to recognise it, there was hardly anything to see. The Mayor later allowed me to photocopy a drawing of the monogram which is kept in their archives and gave permission for it to be reproduced in this book.

The chapel itself belongs to the 14th century but it is in such a state of disrepair that it holds little interest. Some work has been carried out over the decades, including the replacement of the stone vaulted roof with a wooden one, but original frescoes, which were over-painted, have recently been discovered. The Mayor explained that a programme of renovation is due to start in 2008; it's going to take time and a lot of money!

The French are very proud of their heritage and at every opportunity will promote even the smallest church, museum, park or exhibition. Wherever you go you will see signs directing you to something of interest. The tourist brochures describe in glowing terms the treasures and attractions of an area. Inevitably there is the odd occasion when something doesn't quite equal one's expectations. Even so, don't hesitate if something really appeals to your particular interests, take a chance, because, despite my initial reaction to the Roman wash-house and the chapel, and the worn away stone, I'm glad I saw them all. I learned a little more history and met some pleasant and helpful French people of Auvillar.

The building of the Canal des Deux Mers, the construction of new roads, and construction of the railway in the middle of the 19th century, all contributed to taking Auvillar off the beaten track. In 1870 phylloxera struck the vineyards which added to the demise of this formerly affluent village.

Today Auvillar has much to offer its residents by way of art and culture. One of the most popular events is the annual painting competition. In the last week of July the *Viens Peindre Auvillar* competition, 'Come and paint the village', is open to all; amateurs, professionals, even children, with prizes of painting materials and prize money.

On the southern side of the river Garonne, just along the road from Auvillar, you will come to St Nicolas de la Grave. Built in 1135 on a geometric plan, it lies near the confluence of the two rivers – the Tarn and the Garonne. It is the chief town of the district despite the fact that it's not very big, and is a somewhat unprepossessing place at first sight but it has some interesting features.

It is a busy little town, offering its inhabitants and visitors plenty of diversion in the form of markets, fairs, festivals, cycling tours, fishing, canoeing in the river, boat trips, a bird sanctuary, riding centre, *boules,* street painting, concerts, music festivals, exhibitions, heritage days, patchwork club, *brocantes* – those amazing gatherings where one can sell and buy anything deemed second hand goods – and finally the annual Carnival.

What drew me to make a visit was the promise of seeing a chateau of Richard the Lion Heart, still standing; so many of them are nothing but a heap of stones! It doesn't look like a conventional castle, built in red brick and stone, in an E shape with four tall square towers, one at each corner. It has been so changed, renovated and adapted to its present day use, that of the main Administrative Offices of the region, that it is hard to visualise it as it was, even with a romantic and imaginative eye. What is interesting is the fact that, at that time, the bank of the river Garonne was just below the castle, making water transport an important facility. Over the centuries the river course has changed and in the near distance one can see what looks like a large lake, but is in fact a wide stretch of the Garonne, before it bends south towards its source beyond Toulouse.

St Nicolas de la Grave has another famous 'son' – Antoine Laumet – a name you may not recognise at first. He was born in 1658 but sailed to *l'Acadie* in 1683. Acadia was the name given to a colonial territory in Northeast America that included part of Eastern Quebec and other areas. The territory was later divided into the British colonies and eventually became Canadian provinces and American states.

There he adopted a new name Antoine Laumet de La Mothe, *sieur de Cadillac*, squire of Cadillac, 'son of Jean de la Mothe, Seigneur of Cadillac, consultant to the parliament of Toulouse'. In fact his father, Jean Laumet, was a simple magistrate and of no noble birth at all. This was not the only untruth that Antoine Laumet told over the forthcoming years but his innate intelligence, ambitious character and spirit of adventure, led him finally after years of multiple nefarious activities, to a position of some importance and power. Over the years he made several journeys to France, and back to Acadia, and in the service of the King, Louis XIV, he established several forts, one of which in 1701 was Pontchartrain which became the town of Detroit, famous for the automobile industry. He was recalled to France in 1717 and after a brief spell in the Bastille, having been accused of having spoken 'against the government of the State and the Colonies' he was freed. He returned to court, having been shown great clemency and in fact was decorated with the Croix de Saint Louis.

Antoine Lamothe-Cadillac became Governor of the city of *Castelsarrasin*, a town near his native village, where he died in 1730.

It is the name Cadillac which we all now recognise, the famous car, that large, impressive status symbol of the United States.

A museum dedicated to the Cadillac and its history has been set up in St Nicolas de la Grave with the help of General Motors in Detroit. Old and more up to date information is available to the public, with a multimedia hands-on screen to access pictures and facts.

* * *

The economy of the *Tarn et Garonne* is wide-ranging, from craftsmanship to modern technology and agriculture, to say nothing of its hospitality to visitors, which the department has actively developed and is known as 'Green Tourism'.

It is mainly an agricultural department with the growing of fruit of prime importance. This department grows eighty percent of the fruit grown in the whole of the Midi-Pyrénées region. Some few years ago Tarn et Garonne took first place – in the championships for fruit producing departments – for melons; second place for hazelnuts, grapes, pears and apples. They are also renowned for their peaches, nectarines, cherries and kiwifruit. The golden grapes of the variety Chasselas de Moissac, known as the jewels of Tarn et Garonne, produce sweet AOC wines. They are often sold in local markets as dessert grapes and though sweet they are small; we think there's a lot of skin and pips for the reward of a small amount of sweet flesh but they seem very popular with the French. The department is the largest producer of what is said to be the favourite kind of plum eaten in France, that of greengages. The season for the unique plum of the south west, the greengage, or *Reine-Claude*, starts in July until the end of October. They are hand-picked when ripe and are truly, as their French name implies, the queen of summer.

~ *Pigeonniers* ~

As you travel throughout the department you will come across *pigeonniers.* These pigeon houses abound, and though the department claims they are a unique feature of Tarn-et-Garonne, you will find them throughout the south-west.

At one time the privilege of pigeon-keeping was limited to the feudal lords but the French Revolution of 1789 gave the peasant classes the right to benefit from this good source of income. The pigeons were a food source and the manure itself was valuable, used on the *potager,* the individual vegetable plot rather like an allotment, thus yielding better-quality vegetables, to say nothing of the tasty casseroles made from the rich meat. Nothing was wasted; the feathers made bedding and pillows.

The style and construction of the pigeon houses varies according to the wealth of the owner. From the simple to the more ornate, they can be built of brick, stone or half- timbered; round, square, even hexagonal. Some are built as an integral part of the dwelling, others on an open stretch of land and are an architectural delight.

Invitations to take a gastronomic visit, a 'taste and buy' visit, are advertised around every corner, free of charge and with in fact no obligation to buy. But beware, once you set foot in a wine cellar or vineyard for a *dégustation,* you will find it difficult to resist buying just a bottle or two, or three!

Visits to farms are equally tempting. Preserved goose or duck products are expensive but they are absolutely delicious. Many people have an aversion to *foie gras* because of what they believe to be a cruel method of force feeding the geese and ducks. You can visit the farms and see for yourself how they are fed and be assured that those birds love their food! They are greedy creatures. The important thing is to witness the care the farmer takes with his flocks.

Traditional cooking in the south west of France uses duck fat, rather than butter or oil. Conscious today of our health as we are, it is comforting to know that duck fat produces the 'good cholesterol' in our blood. Try potatoes roasted in duck fat – scrumptious and good for you. You can buy pots or jars of the fat in a supermarket or at the farms themselves.

One of the most famous dishes of the south east of France must be the *cassoulet.* The basic ingredients are usually: duck or goose *confit*, pork, Toulouse sausage, *charcuterie,* lingot or butter beans, all cooked in a sauce. '*Confit*', by the way, simply means preserved in duck, goose or pork fat.

There are many French cooks who still argue about what should be in the traditional hearty casserole and so you will find some differences from area to area. Look for the recipe at the end of the chapter on André Coudert in the section Lot et Garonne and consider some of the different ingredients which you can try. Regardless of the variations, *cassoulet* is a rich, warming, nourishing meal, all the better for a good red wine to accompany it, such as Madiran, Cahors or Fitou; in other words a substantial red wine. Incidentally, Toulouse sausage is a speciality in itself; buy it by the metre in Toulouse covered market!

There is nothing more satisfying than shopping in a French market for fresh vegetables and fruit. Camping holidays, or staying in a gîte, give you the ideal opportunity to buy fresh foods and (if not a fluent speaker) to try out your French. Many of the stall holders speak basic English, if not better, and are only too happy to help you.

Most produce can be found throughout the department but some products are a speciality of a particular area.

In Beaumont and Lavit de Lomagne, in the south-west corner of Tarn et Garonne, you will find the larger pearly-white garlic, herbs, strawberries, chestnuts and hazelnuts.

Melons are grown on the sunny, chalky-clay slopes of the Quercy. They are cut in the cool early morning then taken the same day to the packing station. Their firm yet tender orange flesh is full of flavour.

Moissac, and its surroundings, is famous for the 'Chasselas'; the small but sweet golden coloured grape. A new apéritif has recently surfaced – 'Quercy des îles'. Its creator hopes to sell as many as 20,000 bottles in his first year of production, simply by word of mouth. Its base is the juice of the small sweet chasselas grape, blended with rum and vanilla. If the fact that vanilla is said to make one amorous, then it looks as though the sale of this new drink might well enjoy success!

And what of the famous 'black diamond' – Tuber Melanosportum – or as you may know it, the truffle. It needs three conditions for growing: a tree, such as the oak or hazel tree, chalky ground and a climate with a Mediterranean tendency. The truffle has chosen the Quercy region as its favourite location.

It is only in the last seventy years that the truffle collector has used a highly trained dog instead of a sow to find the truffles. The dog, obeying his master's command to stop, is much less likely to damage the precious but rather ugly black lump which he finds by scent. It is harvested from the beginning of November until the beginning of March. Truffle omelette is said to be absolutely delicious, but make sure you have a full wallet before you order it!

Plums, plums, plums! The trees are more numerous than the vines in this area.

La Reine Claude, we know it as the greengage, is a speciality of the south west, grown in the orchards around Montauban and Moissac.

La Prune d'Ente, a purple variety of plum, is also grown here in Tarn et Garonne as in the Lot et Garonne. It is grown mostly for preserving by drying to produce the soft, delicious prunes sold loose on market stalls, packaged for supermarkets or delightfully wrapped in cellophane, beribboned pretty boxes, to buy as gifts. Forget the wrinkled tough, black lumps served with custard at school! The prunes of Tarn et Garonne are the real thing. The word *prune* in French means plum which can be a little confusing. The French word for a prune is *pruneau*.

I have tried numerous recipes using prunes not only in desserts but also in savoury dishes. A family favourite is a sliced pork fillet with a layer of stuffing, and a layer of prunes and walnuts. It not only tastes good, it looks attractive too and has impressed many a guest.

White asparagus is grown in the mid to northern area of the department. Quite different from the green variety more common in Britain, it is milder but nevertheless worth trying. The growing and harvesting of asparagus is a labour intensive, back breaking job but the price in the markets doesn't appear to reflect the demands of the task. Perhaps that's why there are fewer farmers growing it now than a few years ago. Our immediate neighbour is one of the few left in this area who continues to grow it and we see him, and his wife Michelle and two helpers, with their backs bent working in the fields in the spring. But even he is cutting back on the amount that he grows.

Throughout the months of July and August, there are so many exhibitions to enjoy. Both contemporary and classical, oil painting and water colour, painting on glass, sculpture, photographic exhibitions, patchwork and all forms of arts and crafts proliferate. There is even an exhibition on *pigeonniers*, or dove-cots, those architecturally inspired small buildings dedicated to the rearing of pigeons. At *Montauban* there is the permanent exhibition of paintings by *Ingres*.

Within the Circle

~ *Lauzerte* ~

Sitting on top of the hill, Lauzerte – a bastide town and a fine example of urban mediaeval architecture – can be seen from miles around dominating the valley of the small river Barguelonne. It lies within my special circle and is one of the stops on the Saint Jacques de Compostelle pilgrims' way. Visit the *Jardin du Pèlerin,* the pilgrims' garden, to discover the different features of the pilgrimage; retrace the symbolic path, through geography, botany and poetry, in the old French language thoughtfully translated for both the French people of today and for the non-French speaker.

The old houses huddle together on the peak of the hill, the cobbled streets lead into the square with its attractive arcades of light coloured stone, under which you can enjoy a delicious '*grand crème*', a large rich dark coffee with hot frothy milk, perhaps accompanied by a macaroon, the recipe for this sweet renowned local cake a secret still.

Lauzerte stands proudly over the grand views of the surrounding valleys, rich with crops and fruit. Market day is Saturday morning in *Place des Cornières*, the central square; in *Place du Foirail*, in the lower part of the village outside the old walls, is the Farmers' Market each Wednesday.

Lauzerte holds many festivals such as its flower show at the end of April, music and theatre festivals, cultural and natural heritage days in September and *Foires à la Brocante* – antique fairs. The most spectacular festival is '*Les Nuits de Lauzerte*', 'Lauzerte at night' which takes place in August. For two evenings you can amble through the candlelit streets, gazing at the illuminated colourful images projected on the facades of these old buildings. Each year the theme is different and the participants, members of the village as well as artists – dancers, musicians, photographers – interpret the theme in their own particular way, creating an enchanting and magical evening.

~ *Montaigu de Quercy* ~

The former fortified mediaeval village of Montaigu de Quercy belongs to *Bas Quercy*, Lower Quercy, which is frequently referred to as *Quercy Blanc*, White Quercy. This area is formed of layers of hard chalk and calcareous clay, which are almost white in appearance and explains the name. These strata run from the north east towards the south west, forming white plateaux and long valleys which give the countryside a striped effect as though scored through by a huge claw. The French for 'claw' is *serre* and so the area has become geographically known as Pays de Serres.

Montaigu de Quercy perches on a hill in the north of the department, the main town of the *canton* or district. Its white stone buildings and chalky hillside are typical of villages in Quercy Blanc. The village has no fewer than eleven churches, two of which are classified and have 15th to 16th century wall paintings, an old fountain, *lavoirs* - the old wash-houses - and 100 kilometres of paths for the ardent rambler, horse rider or mountain biker.

It's a good holiday centre with its own camping area and facilities. It has a man-made lake for swimming, with a white sand beach, small boats for hire, with tennis, mini golf and picnic areas.

Market day is Saturday with a flourishing trade of local produce throughout the year but the fun engendered during the summer season comes from the mix of visitors as they buy the produce in halting French, ably and kindly helped by the smiling stall holders.

Now read on and meet some of the people who live and work within this section of the circle.

Suzanne Laoué

'Florever'

~ *Flower grower and producer of dried flower arrangements* ~

Though born in Bordeaux Suzanne has lived in various parts of France including Paris, the Massif Centrale (in the wilds of the Cevennes) and in the Aveyron.

'It's no good,' she says, 'I prefer the country, I can't live in a town.' St Vincent, a small village in the Tarn et Garonne department, is definitely 'in the country' and this is where she finally settled and lives, as she puts it, 'a dream come true'.

Suzanne and her partner Jean Paul used to breed goats in the beautiful mountains of the Aveyron and though they loved the countryside and the outdoor life, keeping animals didn't work well with their love of travel. They began to think of other means of making their living in the area. They considered growing plants for medicinal purposes but it soon became evident that this would not produce a viable income. Too many plants were being imported from eastern and south-eastern Europe and they could not compete with their prices.

One day Suzanne noticed someone growing different flowers, for sale both as fresh cut flowers and some dried. As a preferred country dweller here was something she felt they could do and take pleasure in. Growing the flowers was one side of the work, loving the outdoors and working the land would be fulfilling; working with the flowers and making arrangements would add to the interest and pleasure. Suzanne strongly believes that enjoying one's work is vital, otherwise life is not good! So it was that in the mountains of the Aveyron, 800 metres high, they first started growing flowers.

It soon became evident that this was not the right place for such an occupation. Not only was the village very small and therefore had few potential customers, they were miles – or perhaps we should say kilometres – from other communities.

Suzanne goes on to explain why in the beautiful mountains of the Aveyron they could not contemplate this new found dream.

'The weather was not conducive to growing flowers on a large scale; in May there still could be 30cms of snow, the summers were short and it became cold again in early September. The only place we could dry the flowers was in an empty house which was far from ideal. We also realised that the small amount of land at our disposal would not meet our needs.'

Their search for a new location began. It was obvious that the climate was important and that the plot of land should be large enough to be practical and workable. Their criteria were; a flat area, a house, a barn and water. Despite the fact that there were many houses on the market at the time it took a while to find a property that met all their requirements. It was in 1980 that they finally found Sinjou in the department of the Tarn et Garonne; a suitable house and a plot of 3.8 hectares of good chalk land.

'Our first job was to plant trees – 600 of them! The previous owner had cut down everything around the property, except one walnut tree beside the house, this was after we had agreed to purchase!' Suzanne recalls with horror. Suzanne and Jean Paul were devastated. Not only did the lack of trees detract from the beauty of the place but their proposed growing area was unprotected from the elements. Even in south-west France the winters can be cold and more importantly have severe frosts!

'This whole project took time to get established and it's hard to believe now that we learned on the job.' Looking at Suzanne's attractive and colourful flower arrangements today in her display area in the barn where she works, one can hardly believe that she has not done this amazing creative work all her life.

But none of it came about without hard work. Suzanne says,

'When you are self-taught you have to have patience. There's no clock-watching, it's try, try and try again.' Then she says, with an ironical expression, 'First, of course, one must grow the flowers.'

In the beginning the flowers they grew were very small. 'But we thought we were very clever' she laughs. 'It took all day to make one bunch and then people generally didn't appreciate our efforts.'

Suzanne's year begins in September, preparing the ground and sowing the seeds for the next year's blooms, such as poppies and delphiniums. At the end of February the greenhouses must be made ready for sewing in sectioned pots. In April the small plants are transplanted out into the field. The next major task is to set up the watering system. Some plants are irrigated drop by drop into the ground, not on the leaves. Then comes weeding, tilling, and spraying against diseases. At the end of May the cutting of flowers begins and continues until the end of September.

'We are only half way through the process!' she says. 'Once cut, the flowers have to be dried in the large gas-fired drying shed. An electric ventilator channels the warm air moving gently through the full racks of hanging bunches. It takes from one to six days to dry the flowers, the more water the flower contains, for example sunflowers, the longer it takes to dry them. Dried in this way the flowers retain their colour and vibrancy. They are then sorted into colours and types and put into coded boxes to protect them.'

So, there they are, all ready for you to simply place in your vase or to create your own arrangement. But how do you go about finding these wonderful dried flowers or arrangements?

As Suzanne herself says, 'Growing and drying the flowers is one thing but selling is another matter!' Some years ago she sold to shops her beautiful bouquets, posies, tresses, bunches, filled baskets and decorative wall hangings. Whilst she busily put together these floral works of art Jean Paul coped with the commercial side of the business. Then came the influx of dried flowers from India and China. They were cheaper of course but the colours were unnatural, dyes of every hue!

Sadly, truly creative work was, and still is, undervalued and at the time some of Suzanne's business fell away.

Today, in the summer months, Suzanne is to be found each day of the week beside her colourful stall, in one or other of the local markets. Bright freshly cut flowers as well as the multi-coloured dried ones sit happily side by side.

In the winter Suzanne travels to the larger markets in major towns such as Montauban, Toulouse, Cahors and even farther south to Lecture in the department of the Gers, being there from early morning until the evening. Of course she is always in attendance at the Christmas markets with her delightful seasonal decorations.

Many a decorative piece makes its way back to the United Kingdom to grace a table or place in an alcove, not only as something to be admired but also as a memento of a holiday spent in this lovely area of the Tarn et Garonne.

Life isn't all work, she will tell you. But one wonders how she finds the time to read 'a great deal', enjoy music and occasionally play the guitar. And let's not forget Monty her large, friendly, blond *Berger Allemand* - her German Shepherd - who will greet you enthusiastically when you visit her Workshop at St Vincent.

Oh, and by the way, if your French isn't too good, Suzanne speaks excellent English and a little Russian too!

Michelle and Georges Vassal

Farmers; maize, plums, asparagus

~ 'MIROU' ~

The farm stands on the brow of the hill in the commune of Valeilles in the northernmost tip of the department of the Tarn et Garonne, not a kilometre from the border with the Lot et Garonne. To the east the land slopes away with a view across the plain to Tournon d'Agenais in the near distance. On this slope and in the valley below are the plum orchards. To the west behind the farmhouse is a picturesque view across the valley, the land rising up to the hills and the village of Massoulés. On this side of the farm are the fields of cereal crops, and the asparagus beds.

Michelle and Georges are local people - born in this area, living and working here still. Georges' father was a mason in La Croix Blanche in the department of the Lot et Garonne, just a few kilometres away, but Georges has worked in farming from his early teens. He served an extended *Service Militaire,* normally 18 months in those days, due to the Algerian war which interrupted his farming career.

'I did 14 months in France and then 14 in Algeria. I just got caught,' he recounts shaking his head.

Michelle has lived in the farmhouse all her life, where she and Georges live now with Michelle's mother. Michelle's family have owned and run this farm for four generations, and it looks as though it's going to continue in the same family for at least the next two!

It was when Georges married Michelle that they lived with her parents in the large farmhouse. The young couple had their eye on a small property nearby, which Michelle's parents had bought; a house with accompanying land purchased in order to enlarge their farm. Michelle and Georges would have liked to buy the small farmhouse just a little way down the track running between the fields! Sadly it was beyond their means. The little old farmhouse was later sold to another family.

Today this house stands in an acre of garden, much renovated and enlarged over the last forty years, in the hands of four or five different owners, each one making improvements to what was a simple, square, stone farmhouse. The result is a lovely home in the countryside and is now owned by an English couple who appreciate its charm and peaceful setting.

Michelle and Georges still live at the large farmhouse with Michelle's mother, who at 84 makes delicious soups, prepares lunch for the workers coming in at *midi*, and still participates in some of the farm tasks. She is to be found in the barn in the spring; washing, bunching, weighing and packing the asparagus.

Down in the fields, as early as seven o'clock in the morning, during the months of April to June, you will find the little white van waiting to carry back to the barn the crates of newly cut white asparagus. It's quite different from the green variety which is common in

England, and though you can sometimes find the green asparagus in a market it is much less common in this area of France.

Down the track is the first asparagus field and beside it the 'little old farmhouse'. Michelle and Georges can't help but notice it and perhaps they cast a wistful glance at the property now and then, with the thought of what might have been. But they are philosophical, even magnanimous about it – after all they get on well with the English couple – yes, that's us! They enjoy an *aperitif* with us and from time to time have dinner *chez nous* along with the neighbours of this '*petit coin*'. On these occasions Georges likes to get into a political discussion with my husband, whose French is not quite up to a full blown debate, but he keeps pegging away urging Georges on to talk about his feelings and opinions.

Cutting asparagus is a back-breaking task. It's time consuming, labour intensive, sometimes heavy going in wet and muddy weather, and with a very low profit margin.

'So why do you grow it?' I ask Georges.

'There used to be thirty-three asparagus growers in this vicinity, now there are only three – including us. People want it, so we grow it! We have to keep it going, that is as long as the present plants produce a viable crop.'

How long do the plants keep going I wonder? But Georges has already foreseen my question.

'Look,' he says, 'at this field here,' and he points to the mounded rows of earth, 'it'll be finished in a couple of years. The yield diminishes after ten years and the return is poor, so the plants have to be grubbed up.' What then? I'm thinking, but Georges is in full flow.

'My son already has plans, which I'm leaving to him. After all I shall be retiring soon. He's in charge now.' He rubs his hands together and grins, knowing full well that whether he's retired or not, he'll never stop farming. Perhaps he'll have just a little more leisure time which he and Michelle will be able to enjoy.

So their son Serge is in charge now. He makes the decisions about the crops such as maize which is grown for seed, and more recently has decided to grow some for animal consumption. Then there's wheat, soya beans, plums, (more of those later) chickens, and sometimes guinea fowl. I interrupt him here to tease about the *pintades*.

'Those pesky guinea fowl! '*Pourquoi, pourquoi, pourqoi*' they cry all day. When are you going to get rid of them?' I ask.

'Come and teach them to say it in English, if you like,' he laughs.

But 'Why, why, why' doesn't have quite the same ring about it, does it?

'Do you know you can hear them a kilometre away?' Michelle says, hardly able to believe it herself. 'But don't worry, they're only here from October to December. Serge won't let us have them in the summer. He says it's not fair to the neighbours when everyone's outside enjoying the fine weather.'

Michelle is soon back to the subject of Serge, telling me how relieved they are that he is also responsible for all the paper work.

'Oh, so many forms to fill in these days,' says Georges with his hands in the air. He's getting a bit excited and Michelle puts a gentle restraining hand on his arm. Perhaps a change of subject is in order, so I ask him;

'Tell me about the tiny windows in the stone walls, underneath the eaves of the roof one sees in houses in the vicinity. There are some in our house but they have long been glazed, I think.'

'For tobacco drying,' he replies. 'We used to spread the leaves on the floor in the roof space, here in this house. The small windows were for ventilation.'

Yes, now I remember seeing it growing in the fields when I first came to this area but I tell Georges I haven't seen any lately.

'No. Not so many grow it now. There's no money in it. We stopped growing it some years ago.'

'We used to have cows in those days too, you know,' Michelle chips in. 'But there was an over production of milk and in 1980 the government gave out subsidies NOT to produce milk!' she adds with incredulity.

'In any case Serge didn't want cows. It's understandable; how can you produce cereal crops and plums when you've got to be up at dawn to milk the cows and then again in the late evening?' Georges is happy with the decisions his son makes.

So Serge is the fourth generation to be running this farm and his son, Loïc, is following in his footsteps, having already studied at Agricultural College he is now working part time on the farm as he continues his education in mechanics.

'So you see, we shall have a mechanic on the premises - that's important,' says Georges wagging his finger, 'It's essential to have someone who can maintain all the expensive farming equipment we have these days.'

And my goodness, you should see the hangar where such machinery is stored. It's impressive!

Serge's wife, Ghi, is a teacher. She wanted to be married to Serge, but not to the farm, she says. In fairly recent times being the wife of a young farmer was not a girl's first choice! The modern young woman knows full well that the farming life means long hours and few holidays. Besides, educated young women today want their own job and career.

Ghi loves her teaching job and though offered the Headship of the school, which she took up for a while, she decided it was too time consuming and tiring, along with running a home and looking after two children. Farming is not the most well paid work so a regular second salary is an insurance, lessening the worry when the weather is fickle, and enabling them to take the children on educational trips and enjoy good holidays together.

'Let's talk about prunes,' I say to Georges. 'The south west is the centre of the prune producing area of France, isn't it?

'Indeed it is, and we're very proud of it. Of course, it's the variety of plum that's important to produce such good prunes; *la Prune d'Ente.*'

There is some confusion with the French word *prune* which means 'plum'. When the English speak of 'prunes' they mean the dried variety, which in French is a '*pruneau*'.

After picking, the plums are washed, graded for size and moisture content, spread on racks and then slow dried in long, special ovens. Georges and Michelle have their own huge, custom-built ovens to produce both the fully dried plums and the *mi-cuits*, the very moist, lightly dried ones. Serge masterminds the whole process; the harvesting, washing, grading, drying, sorting and packing. Of course, he has had two experienced teachers in his parents, who are still heavily involved. I've watched Michelle sorting and grading the prunes prior to packing - fast and scrupulous!

'So if we want to buy prunes,' I say to Georges, 'we should look for the label '*Pruneaux d'Agen*', is that right?' Georges gives a wry smile. Agen is in the Lot et Garonne department and Georges is a very proud resident of Tarn et Garonne. But he nods in agreement.

Then I tell him;

'Ask any English man what he knows of prunes and he will probably say:

"Black, wrinkly, dried up, eat them stewed with custard. Keep you regular!" Both George and Michelle laugh and nod, but as we all know there's much more to them than that.

Ask a Frenchman and he will say:

'One of the most delicious and versatile of fruits, to say nothing of its health-giving qualities.'

So let's think about the health aspect. Prunes aid digestion and iron intake. They provide slow energy release for sportsmen, contain anti-oxidants and help the elderly absorb minerals and vitamins.

Use them in your cooking; they impart a special and delicious flavour to casseroles. Eat the semi-dried ones raw, like dried apricots, or stuff them with soft cheese as an appetizer. Try the beef casserole at the end of this chapter and if you really can't resist soaking them, try the local method, prunes in eau de vie!

Despite the long working hours, Georges finds time to serve on the Local Council. He's responsible these days for some of the decisions regarding the village school. He also supervises the working requirements of the school canteen. And on Bastille Day, Georges is there, in the *Salle des Fêtes,* making sure everyone, coming from all the villages within the community, is looked after.

Michelle and Georges have had a few short breaks over the years. A week or so in Narbonne, Nice, Montpellier or Luchon.

'Have you been to Luchon?' Michelle asks. I shake my head. 'You must go, it's delightful.'

They envisage more such holidays in their forthcoming retirement, in between the asparagus picking, the maize reaping, and the plum harvest! I wish them well.

Now for a few recipes using prunes.

After my experience of prunes at school many years ago (usually served with glutinous lumpy custard!) it was a while before I began to appreciate the prunes from south west France. Some time after moving in our next door neighbours, Georges and Michelle, gave us some of their own produce and since then I have used them often in cooking in both savoury and sweet dishes.

I am so lucky living right next door to the Vassal family who produce prunes from their marvellous crop of plum trees. As soon as they come out of the ovens I march up the track to the farm to buy my quota. Like most English people I never knew prunes could be so delicious, be used in so many ways, or have such health giving properties. Now I pounce upon any recipe I find which includes prunes.

Prunes in eau de vie

Eau de vie is the French term for a colourless fruit brandy which is distilled from fermented fruit juice. It can be flavoured with any fruit and is very high in alcohol content. So beware! The term *eau de vie* means water of life. Michelle and Georges make this splendid aperitif. The prunes can be eaten on a cocktail stick as a 'nibble' with a glass of wine before a meal, and the eau de vie is in itself a delicious aperitif.

Ingredients
1½ cups of water
2 tablespoons of sugar
1 vanilla bean
350g of pitted *pruneaux d'Agen*, (Agen prunes)
½ cup of eau de vie

Method
Combine the water and sugar in a pan.

Split the vanilla pod and add it and the seeds to the pan and bring to the boil. Stir until the sugar dissolves.

Place the prunes in a clean dry jar and pour the syrup over them.

Refrigerate for at least one week before using.

Refrigerated they will keep indefinitely.

Sometimes this aperitif is made with Armagnac. This too is delicious but more expensive to make.

Pork fillet with prune and walnut stuffing

I cannot give you a precise recipe for this delicious dish. The one I use is in a favourite cookery book of mine and for copyright reasons I may not reproduce it here. So why do I mention it? Perhaps you feel I shouldn't if I can't tell you the full story.

I'll tell you why.

I'm afraid I'm something of a demon when I find a 'new' recipe because I never follow it to the letter. I have my particular and perhaps unconventional methods of cooking and recipes, many of which have come about through years of trial and error. I think most people who enjoy cooking like to experiment from time to time.

If I tell you the basic ingredients and the idea behind the dish then I am sure that those of you who enjoy using your imagination coupled with your culinary flair will produce a delicious meal.

As you can see from the title, you will need pork fillet, known in France as *filet mignon*. You need a good stuffing, some soaked prunes - from the south west of France of course and some walnuts.

How fortunate I am to have a walnut tree in my garden and live next door to the Vassal family who process their plums into delicious prunes. André Coudert, the butcher par excellence featured in the *Lot et Garonne* section, supplies me with the *filet mignon*.

Start by trimming the pork fillet of any fat, then make two cuts through the *filet* lengthways but not quite cutting right through so that you end up with three layers of meat still attached to each other down one side of the filet. Open out the layers ready to spread them with your chosen stuffing.

I make a stuffing of sausage meat with herbs and chopped onions and seasoning but this is where you can use your expertise and particular preferences in herbs.

Spread the stuffing along one layer of the meat. On top of it place rows of pre-soaked prunes - without stones of course, alternated with a row of walnuts. Lay on top one layer of the pork.

Repeat the process with the next layer of stuffing and prunes and walnuts and place the third layer of pork on top.

Tie the whole with fine string in three or four places to secure, wrap in foil and bake in the oven.

When cold wrap in foil or film. Keep in refrigerator until required. Slice to serve with a variety of salads; perfect for a special buffet meal.

This is where I exercise my 'variation on a theme' as my family like it hot! I make a sauce - using any juices which come out of the parcel - and serve the whole, with vegetables. This makes a very nice dish for a dinner party. It looks attractive and it tastes scrumptious!

The following is easy, looks attractive and is delicious.

Poires au vin et aux pruneaux

Poached Pears with Prunes in red wine

Ingredients (Serves 4)

4 just-ripe Williams pears

575 ml red wine

2-3 tbsp sugar

1 vanilla pod, split

8 stoned and soaked prunes or 8 ready-to-eat prunes

2 tbsp *Crème de cassis* (optional)

Method

If using dried prunes soak overnight in a little water.

Peel the pears, using a vegetable peeler – do not cut into the flesh.

In a heavy based saucepan large enough to take the pears comfortably side by side, combine the wine with the sugar and the split vanilla pod. Bring to a simmer over a moderate heat.

Stand the pears side by side in the simmering wine, adding a little water if necessary so that the rounded base of the pears is well covered.

Bring back to a simmer and poach over a low to moderate heat, for about 15 minutes, until just tender basting the top of the pears a few times with a spoonful of the liquid. Add the strained prunes for the last few minutes.

Leave to cool in the liquid for 15 minutes. Lift the pears and prunes from the wine. Place the pears upright on a plate and leave until cold.

Bring the liquid to the boil over a fairly high heat and keep it bubbling until reduced by almost half to a light syrup.

Remove the vanilla pod, rinse, dry and reserve for future use.

If wished, stir the Crème de cassis into the wine syrup.

Leave to cool, stirring occasionally.

Stir in any juices from the pears and prunes.

Serve the pears cold – but not chilled – with a little of the syrup.

We have a few friends who are diabetic and I use the above recipe without the sugar. They tell me it's delicious!

Carbonnade aux pruneaux

Beef and Prune Casserole

You might think it odd to include here a recipe which contains beer, this ingredient being traditionally from the north of France. Red wine would be more what one would expect in a beef casserole of the south west. It is the addition of prunes which makes this dish extra special in my view. This is my version of an old recipe.

Ingredients (Serves 6)

2 tbsp oil

Butter for frying

1.3 kg braising steak, cut into 6 cm chunks, trimmed of fat

225 g thick-cut smoked streaky bacon

3 onions, thinly sliced

2 shallots, sliced

Plain flour for dusting the beef chunks

550 ml brown ale

1 heaped tsp ground dried thyme

2 springs of parsley

2 bay leaves

200 ml light stock

140g of prunes

2 tbsp red wine vinegar

6/8 pieces of toasted bread

1 scant tbsp Dijon mustard

Sea salt and freshly ground black pepper

Method

Heat the oil in a large flameproof casserole, add some butter to the hot oil.

Coat the chunks of beef in flour, season lightly and sauté until slightly crisp, moving them about in the pan so that the pieces don't stick.

In a separate pan blanche the bacon, cut into pieces, in simmering water for 1 minute. Cool and drain well.

Add the bacon and the prepared onions and shallots to the meat and stir well and cook for 2 minutes.

Now pour in the beer, sprinkle over the thyme and a few parsley sprigs and the bay leaves.

Bring to a gentle boil, reducing the heat as soon as the beer bubbles.

Stir well and cover.

Cook for about 1and a half hours over a very low heat or place in an oven on medium to low heat.

Remove from the heat (oven or hob top, whichever you have used) and add the prunes and vinegar, stirring the stew well with the addition of a ladle or two of stock if the mixture looks too dry. (Should be thickened but not like syrup)

Return to a low heat and continue to cook for 20-30 minutes.

Adjust the seasoning and stir well, again add a little stock if necessary.

This dish traditionally has pieces of toast smeared with mustard then layered over the top. It really does finish it off well and in some *cuisiniers'* views it's not complete without it!

6 to 8 triangles of toast buttered lightly on both sides.

Smear with a little Dijon mustard.

Place the toasts over the top of the meat in the casserole.

Now cover completely and cook for a further 15 minutes before serving straight from the casserole.

Slow cooking is the secret to the caramelized flavour of this dish, the beer and vinegar giving it its distinctive tang.

Confit of Prunes

'*Confit*' is a word you will keep coming across in France; it simply means preserved in one form or another, be it crystallized, candied, pickled, preserved in fat, or what we would call in English a 'conserve'.

This *confit* goes well with pork or duck and also with sliced cold meats. In fact, I like it so much I look for dishes I can serve it with!

You can make the *confit* at any time and I have kept it in the fridge for several weeks, quite happily.

Ingredients
150g pitted prunes - *pruneaux d'Agen* of course!

1 large Granny Smith apple

4 shallots, peeled and cut into wedges through the root

275 ml strong dry cider

55ml cider vinegar

1 tablespoon dark brown soft sugar

2 good pinches powdered cloves

1/8 teaspoon powdered mace

Method
Cut the apple into quarters and core then cut into 1 cm slices, leaving the skin on.

Then place all the ingredients together in a saucepan, bring everything up to a gentle simmer. Let it cook as gently as possible, without a lid, for 45 minutes to an hour - stir from time to time - until all the liquid has reduced to a lovely sticky glaze.

And hey presto it's done! Just serve warm with the meat, or equally well it is nice cold like a chutney.

Jacinta Van Wissen

Atelier Aromatiques

Aromatic plants, workshop for essential oils

A change of career from medical science to natural healing may seem like a leap from one extreme to the other. But for Jacinta it was a desire to change her life and a long term interest in plants that led her to make the break.

'For twenty years I was working in nuclear medicine in a hospital, on isotopes with cancer patients. I used to take what you might call 'pictures', not x-rays, I was not a radiologist, I worked with nuclear photographs. I felt I had had enough and I knew I must make a change.' Jacinta is pensive for a few moments and then continues as she tells me of the moment when she left her home in Holland.

'I worked until the very last day before we left for France. On that last day I saw a patient whom I had been treating for some time. He was an editor and I had told him I was leaving. On that last appointment he gave me a book on the French language explaining all the words that have two meanings. I have it still and it has been very useful, as well as a memory of my life before I came here.'

'I had long been interested in organic food and plants and for the last twenty years I have eaten only organic food. I realised this was the direction I wanted to take; 'organic' is the very opposite of nuclear, isn't it?'

As she talks Jacinta herself seems almost surprised at her courageous decision to make such a radical change.

'I come from Holland, a small town between The Hague and Amsterdam, and there I had a garden with vegetables and herbs. I noticed that many of the flowers and herbs had very little perfume and it was this realisation that brought about the idea of finding somewhere to grow herbs organically.'

Twelve years ago Jacinta and her partner visited friends in Montaigu de Quercy. Jacinta knew instinctively that this area was where she could begin again, with her plants. She had only ever been to France once in her life before, but it was enough to convince her that this was the right place to bring her dream to reality.

'We returned home to Holland, sold our house and just came here,' she tells me with some amazement. 'We drove around looking at houses and then one day we found an empty house which was not actually for sale. We spoke to an estate agent; he contacted the owner and he agreed to sell. At the same time I bought a hectare of land, as I saw that the area belonging to the house would not be enough.' Jacinta smiles as she tells of the local farmer who sold her the land and who visits her often now.

On this land where maize and wheat had grown, and before that vines, Jacinta started to plant lavender. All around this area there had been vines; the large, empty house had been the winemaker's home.

'It is not such an old house, built only about a hundred years ago. It was empty for a long time and when we bought it, it needed a lot of renovation to make it habitable. We did it all ourselves,' she says with some pride. She turns to another building;

'This is much older, about two hundred years old.'

We are sitting outside this older building as we chat, with a small cup of black coffee. This older, stone building is some short distance from the main house and it was, at the time of their purchase, in even worse repair. This is where the vineyard workers had lived, in only two rooms, with pigs to keep them company, in a stye at the side of their dwelling. A few metres along was another stone residence, this for the cows.

Jacinta fell in love with all of this; the house, despite its need for restoration, the honey stone out-buildings and the land, she recognised its potential, but at the same time she saw that there was a great deal of work to be done.

134

She lost no time in planting, at first vegetables and flowers, but very soon she understood that the ground was not suitable for such produce.

'It's chalk and very stony here,' she explained. 'It's in the Quercy Blanc area where the soil is very white – hence its name – and so many pebbles. It is, in fact, perfect for growing herbs, I should have realised. After all, when I found it, I knew instinctively that it was right for my purpose. That's when I planted 500 square metres of lavender, which as you can see, is very much at home here.'

Lavender used to be very important in this area but the price began to drop in the sixties. At the same time government subsidies for the growing of wheat were beginning to be handed out to land owners. So naturally, they tore up their lavender and planted wheat.

'I'm glad to say that lavender is coming back,' Jacinta says with feeling.

Many holidaymakers are under the impression that lavender grows only in Provence. It is true that sweeping across the countryside of Provence are countless fields of it; the mounds of lavender planted in long straight rows, with their bright purple flower heads and highly aromatic fragrance, are an unforgettable sight and perfume. Picture post cards and calendars of such scenes abound. Lavender products are for sale everywhere, not just in the department of Provence, but throughout France, proudly labelled with their geographical origin. So it is not surprising that people think 'Provence' when the word 'lavender' is mentioned.

At Belmontet, some half an hour away from Jacinta's home in the Tarn et Garonne, is a lavender distillery, owned and worked by Monsieur and Madame Thevenet. She contacted them to explain her interest in the growing of herbs, in particular lavender, and they kindly helped her. She worked with the owner for a short time and he showed her how he distils the flower heads. This confirmed in Jacinta's mind what she wanted to do.

'I remember thinking to myself, I'm going to make essential oils. And this is, in fact, what I do now,' she says with a firm nod of the head.

'I have to admit, I didn't start very well. I didn't think about the business side of things, such as looking at how I would market my products. I did it the other way round and then thought – how do I know this is going to work? One thing I did do, was to contact the society '*Eco-cort*', which is responsible for the organic control of aromatic and medicinal plants. But I'm a practical person and I learned as I went along. Having a medical background helped and I read a lot, made notes, and I took a course in Provence at *Nyons* which is a centre for distillation. And I'm still learning. My next project is to study aromatherapy.'

That's not the only plan Jacinta has. She would like to organise workshops on herbs and their uses. She has diplomas in massage and reflexology and plans to give treatments. However, all of this must wait a little while. Not until she has finished renovating the small two hundred year old stone house which she describes as 'more romantic', where she intends to live, will she be able to put these ideas into action. In the meantime she lives in Toufailles and uses her caravan, beside the aromatic plants, when she is working on the land. The house renovation is a slow process, but she does have some help now, from her new partner, a Frenchman. Perhaps this is partly why she has integrated so well into the French way of life.

'I have taken up the rhythm of French life and eat my main meal, with a glass of wine of course, at *midi* – the twelve o'clock lunch break. Then like the French I have a siesta. It suits me very well. '

'For the time being I have to content myself with the products I make; that is the several essential oils, such as St John's Wort, and of course lavender.' She is too modest to mention other lavender products such as lavender sachets for drawers and wardrobes and even for placing in the vacuum cleaner.

Jacinta tells me proudly that she is the only grower of organic lavender in the area and that she harvests it by hand.

'It's hard work but it's the way I want to do it.' Again she nods, affirming her intention of doing things her own way.

'When I first started growing lavender I didn't have the right to call it organic. Having applied to the French Control group, *Eco-Cort*, I had to abide by the rules if I was to stick to my original intention of producing organic essential oils. Sadly I had already planted the shrubs, which I could not use as I wished, that cost me a lot of money. Then I had to wait three years, until I could claim my plants were truly organic.'

Jacinta is philosophical about the loss, admitting as she did, that she was too hasty and did not look into the business side of her project before she enthusiastically started planting.

For the time being Jacinta takes her lavender either to the distillery at Belmontet, where she first learned some of the basics of distilling, or she takes it to another distillery in Villeseque in the department of the Lot. It's now that she reveals yet another dream.

'There are two other small producers 5 kilometres away; that makes three of us within 10 kilometres. You never know, perhaps one day we will have our own equipment and share the facilities. But it is something of a dream; the stills are very expensive. For the moment I must concentrate on my house and enjoy what I am already doing.'

I ask Jacinta where she markets her products.

'I share a shop in Lauzerte with three other people. We rent the premises from the *Mairie,* taking turns to man the shop. It's open all year round selling beautiful ceramics, homemade jams and chutneys, dried flower arrangements (yes, Suzanne's work!) goods from Morocco and, of course, my essential oils and other herbal preparations. I am also trying to bring my products into organic shops in the area.'

Other outlets are in Roquecor and Lauzerte markets, a Tea Room in Moissac, and in Bonaguil, near the famous Chateau, which incidentally is every young boy's dream of what a castle is all about and well worth a visit.

Every year *l'Oustival,* the village hall in Montaigu de Quercy, promotes an exhibition of goods during the summer weeks. Artists and craftsmen of many kinds display their high quality merchandise which can be bought or commissioned to a particular specification. Looking for a memento of your wonderful holiday in the south-west? Look no

further, your quest will be fulfilled here. Of course, Jacinta has her place here.

Finally, Jacinta gives me a short lesson in the use of various herbs; rosemary is stimulating; calendula is for massage and dry skin; St John's Wort for sun burn, inflammation, lumbago, sciatica and rheumatism; lavender as a toilet water, for washing wool and silk, as a rinse for greasy hair, and as a household disinfectant. Its use in first aid treatment is well known and it has the largest number of uses of all the aromatic plants. Try honey infused with lavender oil for a sore throat. The honey is soothing and the lavender oil is healing.

And the word itself - 'lavender'? It comes from the Latin 'lavandum', a part of speech of the verb 'lavare', meaning to wash.

I have learned so much today and I thank Jacinta for her willingness to talk to me about her life.

Naturally Jacinta likes to use organic vegetables and told me of her simple recipe for a Dutch traditional soup, which she says 'Is a complete meal in itself for the winter.'

Dutch Traditional Soup

Using whatever amounts of the following ingredients suit you, make up the soup according to your preferences.

Ingredients for Winter Soup

Dried split peas - soaked	Celery
Potatoes	Celeriac
Carrots	Leeks
Onions	Bay leaf
A hock of pork for flavour	
Salt and pepper	

Method

Soak the peas overnight.

Cook the hock in boiling water, allow to go cold and skim off the fat which has settled on the top.

Meanwhile peel the vegetables and chop into small pieces.

Place the chopped vegetables in the pork stock, add the bay leaf and season according to taste, and cook until tender.

The soup can be eaten with the vegetables left in chunky pieces or liquidised to a smooth soup.

It seems fitting to talk about herbs in relation to Jacinta as she grows so many for medicinal purposes, alongside her lavender, here in the Tarn et Garonne. So you may be wondering why I talk of *Provençal* herbs when this book is about the south west of France. After all herbs will grow anywhere with the right climate and care but we in England have come to associate herbs with the region of Provence.

Herbes de Provence

Provençal Herbs

There's nothing new in using herbs in English cookery; no self-respecting Mediaeval cook, right through to Victorian cooks, would have been without a good supply of fresh herbs. But the use of them somehow fell away for a while, except perhaps in country cooking, and now it is fashionable to use herbs again, especially those from Provence.

A pack of Provençal herbs is usually made up of a combination of some or all of the following; thyme, sage, parsley, rosemary, savoury, basil and bay.

I include them here in this section on lavender because not many people realise that you can blend lavender flowers with the usual mix as listed above.

This is a mix that goes well with chicken. Try it with this next recipe.

Chicken Escalope with Herbs

Ingredients

Olive oil

Skinned chicken breasts.

2 teaspoons of Lavender enhanced herbs*

2 to 3 teaspoons of plain flour

Salt and pepper

Method

First grind the lavender with the herb mixture and flour in a coffee grinder or with a pestle and mortar. Set to one side.

Place the chicken pieces between greaseproof paper and flatten to resemble escalope, about 1cm to 1½cm thick.

Rub a little olive oil onto both sides of each escalope and sprinkle with some of the herb mixture, also on both sides.

Cook in olive oil in a skillet or heavy based frying pan.

Very tasty cooked on a barbecue!

*Consult the notes on the use of lavender in cooking under *Crème Brulée à la lavande,* which follow.

Crème Brulée à la lavande

Lavender Cream Brulée

I first tasted lavender *crème brulée* at the Chateau de l'Hoste in St Beauzeil made by Guy Hérault, the Chef. I have never had a brulée to match it.

You can use your own recipe but first there are a few points to which you should pay attention:

Do not use lavender flowers from a florists shop, garden centre or nursery.

Often these plants have been sprayed with an insecticide which is harmful if ingested.

You can use lavender flowers from your own garden as you will know whether it is safe or not, or you can purchase Culinary Lavender.

If harvesting your own lavender flowers choose the freshest looking flower heads with a good head of flowers. The fresher the flower the more flavoursome it will be.

Gather them as near to the time as you wish to use them and if you have cut them as stems place them in water until needed.

Lay the blooms in water to remove insects or soil then dry on kitchen paper by dabbing gently.

I shall not give you a specific recipe for the brulée, consult any good recipe book, as we all have our favourites. Suffice it to say that all you need to do is infuse the cream with the lavender flowers as follows:

Method

Place the cream in a heavy saucepan and add the lavender flowers.

Heat just to simmering point and then remove the pan from the heat.

Leave to stand for five minutes to allow the lavender to infuse with the cream.

Strain the cream through a fine sieve to remove the flowers and continue with your usual recipe.

Eric and Lisa Trepp

Hoteliers and Restaurateurs

Chateau de l'Hoste

Set in a park of about five hectares, with century old trees in its grounds, is Le Chateau de l'Hoste. Historical records make reference to a 'sort of fortified house', in connection with the villages of St Beauzeil and Roquecor. It is possible that this building was constructed round about the 15th century, the clue being in the name itself which has echoes of military and feudal times. A vassal had to render service to his 'host' (the lord), generally for a period of forty days. The lord would call on the barons and sometimes the vassals but occasionally the vassal would refuse the service called for. In this instance he who refused was liable to the confiscation of all possessions resulting from his position as vassal. In the case of the Chateau de l'Hoste the service was due to the lord of St Beauzeil, or to the lord of Roquecor. Much later, it became, during the 18th century, a *gentilhommière*, a small country seat or manor house.

It has passed through several families. At one time belonging to a member of the *de St Croix* family, who it is thought, was a general under Napoleon. Finally it was converted into an *ostellerie* and has been owned by several different hoteliers.

Six years ago Eric and Lisa Trepp bought the hotel. Its décor and ambience were 'not so much old fashioned' Eric says, as 'going downhill.' A programme of refurbishment throughout the building has restored it to a place of charm and comfort.

Eric Trepp is from a Swiss-French background but was born on the Côte d'Azur. During the early years of his work he met Lisa in Morocco, who was working in the travel industry. It was in 1990 that they moved to the Ile de Réunion where they managed a group of hotels and later formed the consortium Anthurium Hôtels, based in the Indian Ocean and in France. This group consists of like-minded independent hoteliers whose endeavour is to create an hotel of character where authenticity, high quality service, tradition and good taste are words not too grand to describe their aims.

Each hotel, though adhering to the common ideals, displays the personal touch of the owners.

It was in the year 2000 that Eric and Lisa decided to return to France for the benefit of their children. They toured the country in search of the right place to settle down so that their two children could discover and become familiar with France, learn to appreciate it and enjoy new experiences.

'We came to this area on the edge of the Tarn et Garonne and thought it attractive countryside; it was calm though not isolated, with good communications and interesting towns not too far away, such as Villeneuve-sur-Lot and Agen.'

'When we first looked over the hotel it was winter, cold and damp, and the Chateau didn't look at its best. It was just before Christmas and the hotel was closed, they had to open it up especially for us to view it. Despite the bleakness, I felt the charm of the place, the stones seemed to breathe history and mystery. I had a vision of what it could be but both Lisa and I realised there would be a lot of work involved to achieve that.'

Even so they took it on.

'It has been a lot of work, hasn't it? But you set about it straight away,' I say with admiration, having known the hotel long before Eric and Lisa took over. Gradually over a number of years I had with some sadness watched the onset of its fading appeal and experienced its lacklustre atmosphere. But I continued to dine there from time to time, for I too felt the magic of the place.

'We set to work, a little at a time. And we've kept going. But you know, there's lots more to do,' Eric says reconciled to the fact, nevertheless he speaks with enthusiasm.

'What did you feel had to be tackled first?'

'Oh, the first thing we did was change the bedrooms,' Eric says with feeling.

'New curtains, pictures in the bedrooms and some nice pieces of furniture were chosen to give the rooms some character. We have an ongoing programme of converting some of the second floor rooms into luxury bedrooms, or mini suites. Such renovation is complemented by the appeal of the beams already in place; these old timbers lend atmosphere and make an ideal setting for a romantic weekend.'

'We then thought about the hallway. First impressions are so important, aren't they? So we decided to brighten up the entrance. We bought some old traditional furniture for the hall to give it an air of authenticity. One must appreciate that you have to give a building such as this some significant pieces of furniture in recognition of tradition and to give the place an atmosphere of both stability and the passing of time.'

The chosen pieces do indeed look as though they have always been there.

'We took away some large doors which led into the bar and reception area. We didn't like the closed off atmosphere that they gave. We put new furniture in the bar/lounge to make it look like a normal comfortable sitting room. Our aim is to welcome people into the hotel, not as passing clients, but to make them feel *chez eux*, you know, at home.'

Eric continues on this theme of unpretentious comfort in charming surroundings.

'We want the ambience of this hotel and restaurant to be one of ease, not just a place of accommodation and somewhere to eat, but a place to want to come to because of its charm, its comfort, its friendliness, a place to spend leisure time. All of this set in this attractive south west area of France, of picturesque

scenery and of historical interest.'

It's quite obvious that Eric and Lisa are passionate about making Le Chateau de l'Hoste more than a memory in peoples' minds. Their colourful brochure says 'our clients are our privileged guests'; this is a sincere wish that their 'guests' will feel at home and when they leave, will do so with a heartfelt desire to return before too long.

Eric and Lisa have two children. Having been in the hotel industry all their married lives I wondered how it had affected their family life.

'The children were born into the life and have known nothing else,' Eric tells me. 'Because we were working in the hotel the children were always there, 'at home' so to speak. We always made time for them, eating together as a family, and we had some help to keep things running smoothly.'

Alexandre is now 22 and Stephanie 18 and I wonder, after being immersed in the hotel business, if they will follow in their parents' footsteps. But I discover quite soon that both of them have done work experience in the hotel and Stephanie is about to leave for Switzerland for a year's training.

We come back to the renovations and Eric and Lisa's ongoing ideas for improving the Chateau.

'There's still work to be done. The roof needs renovating and the woodwork needs attention. But of course these things take time. We have to do what we can year by year without breaking the bank!'

At this moment in our conversation Valerie comes into the room.

Valerie Maronnier is Directrice du Chateau de l'Hoste. I had asked Eric about the special evenings of entertainment held in the hotel.

'Oh that's Valerie's doing,' he said. 'Valerie was responsible for starting up the programme of our special evenings and she now organizes them on a regular basis; themed evenings, romantic dinner dances, music hall, such as Carribean or Brazilian themes, singers etc.'

Valerie explained that the music hall shows are held in a special venue of the hotel and are held only about once a year. They are of course totally in French, sometimes with a comedian, difficult for non-French speakers, so the dining room is closed on these occasions. But conscious of not wanting to disappoint clients these special evenings are not too frequent.

'I think I'd better talk to Valerie too!' I say.

'Indeed you must,' Eric says, leaving us for a while.

And so Valerie begins to tell me about her job as hotel Manager. Her duties are numerous. She is responsible for all the personnel under her constant care, as well as the recruitment of all the young trainees and apprentices in the hotel, for whom she is accountable, making sure that they are following their particular course of training.

'There are two types of training courses,' she begins to explain to me. 'One for French students, and another for students from the rest of Europe; and two different approaches to a final qualification.' It all sounds rather complicated but Valerie obviously knows the systems well.

'It seems like an awful lot to keep your eye on,' I comment to Valerie, to which she replies, 'Yes, but it's my job and I'm happy doing it.'

There is another responsibility that Valerie undertakes and that is the ever-changing display of art in the dining room. I had commented on the variety of styles of pictures ranging from traditional to modern, oil, water-colour, line drawing, many of which are by local artists. In conjunction with the artists Valerie organises these *expositions*. On each visit I look forward to seeing what is currently being exhibited.

Having trainees and apprentices, the difference between the two being partially explained by Valerie, is a necessary part of the hotel. Eric explained:

'We're a team, all at different levels of expertise. If we, as hoteliers, want the business to go on then we have to make sure we have the staff, qualified staff, in the future. So when it comes to taking on these youngsters, my interest is not entirely altruistic.' He grins, adding 'Of course I care about their training and well being as well.'

It's quite obvious that the day to day running of the le Chateau is teamwork with Eric and Lisa at the helm. And on board this 'ship' is Guy Hérault, the Chef, whose culinary expertise is vital to the success of any restaurant.

I have the pleasure of talking to Guy, who Eric says, he had 'the good fortune to inherit when I took over the hotel six years ago.'

Guy has been the Chef here for several years.

'I came from the Paris region, trained there and then went to Geneva, to work in a grand Casino. Quite different from here at the Chateau, which I have to say, I much prefer. I love my work here, it's varied.'

'What style of cooking do you prefer?' I ask Guy.

'My own. I don't mean that in a conceited way at all, but I like experimenting with flavours, discovering new dishes that way; and I use my imagination. I suppose it's a mixture of classic and being a little innovative. And of course, in an area like this, I embrace *la cuisine du terroir* - you know, using traditional recipes and local produce - according to the season. One could never ignore duck, *foie gras*, prunes and asparagus here in the south west of France.'

Like Eric who believes in apprenticeships and training future hoteliers, Guy believes in teaching the young to cook and to this end he spends time in the local primary schools every year. He has three children of his own and knows just how to hold the pupils' interest. He holds a 'workshop', cooking amongst other things interesting vegetables, including some old-fashioned ones, he says;

'I want the children to discover new flavours and textures of foods.'

The children participate in the cooking and afterwards have a tasting session.

'We sometimes make things they can do at home, for instance prunes in chocolate, and almond paste. Oh they liked that!' So would I, I tell him.

Guy has yet another string to his bow. In the recently renovated and updated kitchen Guy has, for the last two years, run three-day cookery courses. The clients, often different nationalities, from far and wide, stay in the Chateau and attend his morning classes in the hotel kitchen, from 9 to 11 am. On the first day he teaches them how to produce *foie gras*, but first what to look out for when buying duck liver, how to prepare it and then to cook it. On the second day, he concentrates on salmon and on the third day it's *la patisserie;* delicious, mouth-watering pastries!

In the afternoon of each of these three days, they make forays into the countryside, accompanied by Guy of course, including visits to local *caves* – the wine cellars – for the inevitable *dégustation!*

No wonder Eric and Lisa were happy to find that Guy was the resident Chef when they took over *Le Chateau de L'Hoste.*

Try Guy's recipe for *filet de bar.* Delicious!

Eric and Lisa's expertise and commitment is bringing results. Le Chateau de L'Hoste now deservedly has three stars.

'We are seven constant members in our main team,' says Eric, 'along with others who come and go as they complete their training. The hotel is open all year round, except on Christmas Eve. It's obvious that most people want to be at home on Christmas Eve. And of course we have to think of our staff who deserve some time off,' Eric explains, 'after all they will be on duty the next day – for lunch on Christmas Day.'

New Year's Eve follows all too soon; *Reveillon,* an evening celebrated in style by the French, and with much enthusiasm. A very special dinner is served at the Chateau, devised and cooked by Guy and his team, with music during the serving of an aperitif and through dinner, followed by dancing all evening. Then comes New Year's Day lunch, served with a celebratory glass of Champagne.

And so another year begins. Who knows what transformations and renovations this coming year will bring as Eric and Lisa continue to perfect their 'home from home' Hotel.

From Guy Hérault

Chef at Le Chateau de L'Hoste

Filet de Bar au Fenouil

Fillet of Bass with Fennel

Guy did not give precise quantities for this recipe, believing that simplicity is the key to success with a good fish, such as bass.

'A good cook must try new things, new ways and learn to experiment,' he said. 'Try it yourself,' he added.

I did - it was good. Best of luck!

Ingredients (Serves 4)
4 filets of bass

Olive Oil for frying

Fennel bulb

Lemon juice

Fish stock - enough to cover the fennel pieces.

Dry White wine

Aniseed powder

A few olive leaves

Method
Trim the fennel bulb and cut in half lengthways through the root. Cut each half into six wedges. Place in the boiling fish stock and simmer for 20 minutes. Lift out, drain and set aside.

Fry the bass filets in a little olive oil in a large frying pan. Place on a plate to keep hot.

In the same pan reheat the fennel pieces until just slightly coloured underneath. Remove and keep hot.

Arrange the fennel pieces on a serving platter, lay the bass fillets on top, sprinkle a little aniseed powder over and around and then pour over the lemon juice.

Decorate with a few olive leaves for colour.

Serve at once.

Part 3

Department of the Lot

Une Surprise à Chaque Pas

A surprise at every step

The department of the Lot is indeed full of surprises, not least of which are its scenic villages. It's also a land rich in history and as you enter the department from the Tarn et Garonne border en route to Montcuq, more of which later, a welcoming sign boasts '420 Historic Monuments and protected sites'.

Le Quercy

Map of the Region of Quercy reproduced with kind permission of
the artist Christian Verdun: www.christian-verdun.com and
Claude Lufeaux of Quercy.net

Neighbouring the region of Aquitaine, the department of the Lot was established in the northern part of Quercy, an old royal province, which stretches down into the department of the Tarn et Garonne. The ninety six departments of France were created after the Revolution, the Lot taking its name from its main, very long river.

The name Quercy originates from the name of the Gauls – the Cadurci – who were living here when the Romans arrived in this area.

Quercy province, although no longer an official region or department of France, is the term still used to describe a general area, extending from the slopes of the Massif Central to the Aquitaine Basin. It encompasses the whole of the department of the *Lot*. It is linked administratively to the Midi-Pyrenees Region.

Quercy is a speleologists' paradise, for here in this area abound caves, grottoes, chasms, gorges and canyons, underground water ways and Paleolithic wall paintings.

The gastronomy of the department is traditionally *paysanne,* but don't be misled into thinking that it is rough and ready country food; far from it, it is wholesome, nutritious, fresh farm produce. Lamb, poultry, goats cheeses, walnuts and truffles feature on any menu, not forgetting of course the rich dark red wine of Cahors.

Six rivers flow through this department, the principal three are the Lot, the Dordogne and the Célé. Over millions of years as they have wound their way through the limestone plateau of the Causse, cutting and shaping, they have created valleys and canyons. Steep sided white rocks rise out of the valleys. In some areas literally millions of trees cover the hills; in the valleys, the rivers flow peacefully.

Other than its capital Cahors, there are no large towns. Throughout the department the population is low and it is therefore uncrowded.

Divided into five geographical areas (which are described separately in the following pages) it is a department of contrasts waiting to be discovered. Out of France's total of 151 *Plus Beaux Villages de France*, the department of the Lot claims six of them.

~ *Pays de Cahors et du Sud du Lot* ~

~ *The land of Cahors and south of the Lot* ~

This is the south west corner of the department. The town of Cahors, the administrative capital of the department, rests on a peninsular in a loop of the river Lot.

Along the gentle meandering river are the rows and rows of vines, which since Roman times have produced the famous 'Black Wine' of Cahors. It is a dark, intense red – in fact it exists only as a red wine. Yes, rosé and white wines are produced in the Lot but they cannot be classed as *Cahors Appellation d'Origine Controlé*. Nevertheless, don't pass them up. The rosé is one of my favourite wines, sipped as an aperitif on a warm summer evening or accompanying light meals such as warm goat's cheese salad with walnuts and frizzled *lardons*, those delicious morsels of bacon which one can buy conveniently ready chopped in packs.

~ *Cahors* ~

The city of Cahors is rich in history. It was a cultured and wealthy city, founded in the 1st century BC, at that time known as Divona Cadurcorum. The Arc of Diane, a stone arch, is the sole evidence of its former Gallo-Roman thermal baths, which were supplied by an aqueduct bringing water from the valley of the Vers. The name is alleged to honour the original town, built as a sanctuary around the sacred spring of Divona, which is now known as the *Fontaine des Chartreux.*

Nestling in a loop of the river Lot, Cahors as explained earlier is built on a peninsula, a *presqu'île* - almost an island. At one time there were three impressive bridges, two of which were replaced, but the third, built in the 14th century, is one of the most splendid bridges you will ever see. It is the only fortified bridge in the world with three towers and is classed as a major site in the UNESCO World Heritage list. The *Valentré* bridge is the symbol of Cahors.

There's a fascinating legend concerning this famous bridge, also known as the Devil's Bridge. Its construction began in 1308 but was still incomplete in 1378. The slow progress of the building gave rise to the *Légende du Diable,* The Devil's Legend. The architect of the bridge, growing old and weary of the lengthy time it was taking to finish the work, sold his soul to the devil in exchange for his help. The construction was nearing completion when the architect thought

of a way of releasing himself from the pact. To fool him, the architect insisted that Satan must fetch the water that the workers needed and so he provided him with a sieve to do the job. Satan soon recognised defeat in the impossible task. In retaliation he took out the last stone laid at the top of the central tower. The masons put the stone back in place the next day but each night Satan removed it. It was during the restoration of the bridge in 1879 that Paul Gout, the then architect, filled the gap with a stone on which was sculpted a tiny devil trying frenziedly to pull it out. The architect had the stone placed at the top of the central tower, in order to keep the legend alive. Since then not a single stone has been removed by Satan, as in his belief this other sculpted devil was taking his revenge.

Cahors is an historian's paradise. In the 13th century the town flourished due to the arrival of *les Caorsins* from Lombardy they were bankers and eminent international business men. Their influence and power is evident in the facades of the mediaeval residences and dwellings of the devout aristocrats and the merchant bourgeoisie, also in the shopping arcades, workshops, twin bay and tracery windows on the upper floors of the houses. Over three hundred of them have been preserved in the old quarter. Take a walk along the *rue droite*, the *rue Nationale*, the *rue du Château du Roi* and *rue des Soubirous* in the old part of the town, all to the east of *Boulevard Gambetta*.

Born of Italian immigrant parents in Cahors in 1838, Léon Gambetta was the founding father of the Third Republic of France. He declared that to govern the French 'one must use violent words but moderate actions'. He was the instigator of the radical programme of Belleville, in 1869, which called for free, secular and compulsory education; freedom of the press and votes for all. He asserted that *l'avenir n'est interdit à personne,* the future is denied to no-one. On the 4th of September

1870, he escaped from the siege of Paris in a balloon. He virtually ruled France until its defeat by Germany in 1871. His statue stands proudly in the main square in the centre of the town. You will come across streets in many towns in France, not just the department of the Lot, named in his memory, acknowledging his political career and defence of democratic values.

~ *La Cathédrale de Saint Etienne* ~

St Stephen's Cathedral, is a bit of a mix and muddle of styles, the result of several building campaigns embarked upon over the centuries between the 12th and 17th. Restoration work carried out in the 19th century highlighted the differences.

The nave and the North door are both Romanesque, 1120 and 1150 respectively. The apse begun in the 12th century was rebuilt in the late 13th century. The new Gothic choir is said perhaps to be one of the major southern Gothic constructions attributed to Jean Deschamps, who was credited with introducing the northern Gothic style into the south of France. In the early 1300s a huge western tower was built, creating a new façade. The destruction of houses clustered around the edifice opened up a new square – the *Place Chapou.* Interior alterations continued throughout the 15th and 16th centuries adding chapels.

It was in 1506 that work on the cloisters began, becoming an excellent example of flamboyant Gothic architecture. In the north gallery a bust of a pilgrim, characterised by a scallop shell, is carved on a vault-spring. On a sculpture at the northern end of the west gallery one can see a garland of scallop shells.

Cahors is close to one of the main routes of the Pilgrim's Way to Santiago de Compostela and was an important staging post for pilgrims. There a pilgrim could find lodgings, medical care and assistance in specially built 'hospitals' all funded by public charity.

Just off the *Boulevard Gambetta*, behind the building housing the Municipal Information Office, is *Place Galdemar.* Here was Saint Stephen's Hospital which is mentioned in texts as early as the 11th century. From 1253 onwards it appears to have become known as Saint James' Hospital, this one having its own cemetery. Later in the 14th century it was given a Chapel intended for the sick.

Pilgrims could also find lodgings outside the city walls. In the 7th century monasteries of the Abbey of Saint Amans and Abbey of Our Lady existed, and later in the 12th century the Benedictine priory of Our Lady de la Daurade was added to the group.

~ *Les Jardins Secrets* ~

You can find the Secret Gardens of Cahors by following the designated routes marked by polished brass studs engraved with acanthus leaves, set in the pavements. The creation of these twenty-nine gardens began in 2002. In the old part of the town in abandoned or neglected corners, small areas of garden based on different themes have been created, growing plants typical of the Middle Ages, recalling the floral past. In mediaeval times vegetables were perceived as divine beings and the *potager*, the kitchen garden, a place demanding respect and reverence. In following the garden route the visitor has the added pleasure of experiencing some of the history and architecture of the old parts of the town.

A delightful scheme, named *Villes et Villages Fleuris*, operates in France for rewarding towns and villages for their floral displays. It promotes and encourages town councils to take pride in their open spaces and create floral displays for the pleasure of their residents. The reward is symbolic, ranging from one to four 'flowers' on a panel as you enter the town, depending on the quality of the displays. Cahors proudly displays the top grade sign of four flower symbols.

Visit if you have time:

- the Resistance Museum

- the Wine and Truffle Museum

- the superb 8 metre high Salle is lined with old books and has a wooden spiral staircase leading to works from the 15th to 19th century.

There are so many sights worth visiting in the city of Cahors, it can take all day to amble round just a few of them if you want to do them justice. It's not surprising after experiencing the art and history of this still smart and charismatic town, that the accolade of *Ville d'Art et d'Histoire* status in 2005 was bestowed with good reason.

The only way to get the most out of this historically remarkable city is to arm yourself with a good guidebook, allow yourself plenty of time and treat yourself to a delicious lunch in one of the many excellent restaurants.

~ *Parc Naturel Regional des Causses du Quercy* ~

~ *The Regional Natural Park of the Quercy Plateau* ~

Across France there are 44 impressive natural regional parks. They are managed with the aim of preserving the plant and animal life of the region and safeguarding the history and heritage of each place. Some seven of them have hotels, known as *Hôtels au Naturel*, which uphold traditional working practices, source their products locally and protect the environment. One of the parks is the *Parc Naturel Regional des Causses du Quercy.*

This is the central and largest area of the Lot department. Its northern part reaches as far as the river Dordogne and south to the department of the Tarn et Garonne and the slopes of the Quercy Blanc. This huge and unusual natural park is at the heart of the department of the Lot.

Wishing to preserve the harmony and riches of their land and to enhance the status of their natural and cultural heritage, the people of the *Causses du Quercy*, willingly agreed and worked alongside their elected local councillors to create in 1999 the *Parc Naturel National des Causses du Quercy*, which encompasses ninety-seven communities.

Wooded hillsides, valleys without water, short valleys and basins dug out by erosion, one rarely sees water, but it is there, circulating underground in immense networks of galleries. Natural wells, chasms and caverns give access to this water.

Up on the chalky plateau of dry grass is pasture for the ewes that produce the milk for that distinctive flavoured sheep's cheese, simply known as *brebis*, which means 'ewe'.

Here you will see the *moutons à lunettes noires du Quercy* – the sheep which appear to be wearing black spectacles! A delightful legend lives on of how this type of sheep developed its black eye patches.

It is long ago, as the story goes, that sheep were introduced to graze freely on the slopes of the *Causse*. Alas, the animals did not thrive; gradually they wasted away with an eye infection. Today it is known as conjunctivitis. The story is told of how a shepherd was in the habit of protecting the eyes of his sheep with a dark-coloured but transparent scarf against the strong reflection of light on these white hills. One night, he took the charcoal from the fire where he had cooked his dinner; he had had an idea! With this charcoal he encircled the eyes of the sheep. The sheep began to get better and the disease diminished, so much so, that the treatment was applied as a preventative measure.

From then on, when the sheep produced young, the ewes gazed at their mirror image – their lambs too carried the black eye circle! The legend asks; from the moment of creation had not the Creator foreseen mutation? Nature is such, that all future sheep on the *Causse* naturally bore the black eye circle. The *Caussenarde* race of sheep was born.

Stone shepherds' huts of different styles, sizes and shapes, are found throughout the Lot, not only in the area of the National Park. Conical, pointed or domed, the roof is sometimes low sometimes tall. Some of them have a 'wheat sheaf' on the roof having various symbolic meanings; traditional beliefs, sexual symbol of the fruitfulness of the land and the fertility of the breeding of stock. These stone buildings are called by different names; bories, cazelles, gariottes, capitelles, and have an open entrance and offer protection for the shepherds from the inclement weather.

~ *Saint-Cirq Lapopie* ~

In this the largest of the five areas of the Lot, is one of the *Plus Beaux Villages de France,* Saint-Cirq Lapopie. André Malraux, the French writer and political figure, called this one of the most beautiful spots in the world of artists.

Henri Martin, the post-impressionist artist, adored to paint views over the winding river *Lot.* André Breton the poet, essayist, critic, editor and one of the founders of the Surrealist Movement, a movement in visual arts and literature between the two world wars, lived in *L'Auberge des Mariniers,* the Boatmen's Inn in the village. He proclaimed one day that *il avait cessé de se desirer ailleurs* – he no longer wanted to be anywhere else.

Hanging on a cliff-side about one hundred metres above the river *Lot*, this village is one of the most striking of the Lot valley.

In the Middle Ages four feudal dynasties shared the town of Saint-Cirq Lapopie; the Lapopies, the Gourdons, the Cardaillacs and the Castelnaus. This sharing explains the numerous chateaux and fortified houses which dominated the village and acted as a defence and security for the villagers. First climb up the rough path to La Popie Rock, the name of the breast-shaped highest point on the cliff, and walk among the foundations of what was the fortress keep. Appreciate Saint-Cirq Lapopie's commanding position and admire the extensive view. Then amble through the narrow streets, formerly often closed off with fortified gateways, up and around and in between the narrow houses, their half-timbered or stone facades dating back to the 13th to 16th century. The houses of the well-to-do were separated by an *entremi;* a narrow space through which the rain flowed and washed away the used and often foul water from the house.

Hints of artisans' workshops, which made Saint-Cirq Lapopie rich, can be recognised in the arcades in the streets, where tanners, wood turners, leatherworkers worked and wooden taps for barrels and casks were made.

 At the foot of La Popie rock you will see mills, locks, dams, quays and towpaths running alongside the river, evidence of the flourishing river transport which brought wealth to the Lot valley. The drive along the riverside road from Cahors to Saint-Cirq Lapopie is a treat in itself but if you want to relax and get the most out of the scenery you can cruise on the gentle river, glide through time by taking a boat from the quay beside the *Valentré* bridge in Cahors.

~ *Cabrerets* ~

Having crossed the river Lot, almost due north of Saint-Cirq Lapopie, near the confluence of the river Célé (a tributary of the Lot) and the small river Sagne, is the attractive village of Cabrerets, with its fascinating ruins. The village nestles at the foot of the *Roche-Courbe* cliffs with the quixotic ruins of the troglodyte Devil's Castle, said to have existed since the 8th century, emerging unexpectedly from a natural wall. This chateau, also known as the *Château des Anglais*, hangs on the vertical cliff side. It still has a tower and a mullioned window and is mentioned in records as early as 1259 and was at first the residence of the lords of Barasc. In 1380, during the Hundred Years War, it fell into the hands of those in the service of Les *Anglais d'Aquitaine* remembering that this area was still under English rule, which thus explains the origin of the name of the château. Some ten years later it was retaken, the 'outlaws' were ousted and most of the castle torn down.

Just a little farther south of the village is the impressive 13th century castle of Gontaut-Biron which dominates the Céré valley. One can see its huge corner tower which overhangs the road 25 metres above but sadly not the balustraded terrace and interior courtyard as the castle is not open to the public. It belonged to the Marshall-Duke Charles de Gontaut-Biron, a so called friend of King Henry IV but who later betrayed him.

The museum in the village shows the life of Quercy people during prehistory and gives a deeper understanding of one's visit to the Pech Merle Grotto. Surrounding the caves is the Montclar Forest described as having 'a wild beauty'.

~ *Grotte de Pech-Merle* ~

Three kilometres from Cabrerets is the fascinating cave of Pech-Merle. Unlike the perhaps more famous caves of Lascaux in the Périgord, here you can see the real thing.

It is thought to have been some kind of temple to the people of 20,000 years ago.

Lost in time it was rediscovered in 1922. The Priest of Cabrerets, Abbé Lemozzi, was a cave explorer and a scholar of prehistory. His talks to two 14 year old schoolboys inspired them to explore a small hole which was known to have been used as a hiding place during the Revolution. The boys crawled along a slippery trench, sometimes blocked by limestone but at last they came to a huge chamber. To their amazement they saw wonderful wall paintings and carvings.

Abbé Lemozzi then explored the cave and with his knowledge and understanding realised that it was an underground temple. He described it as 'a Sistine chapel of the Causses plateau, one of the most beautiful monuments of the pictorial art of the Paleolithic age'. It was very soon opened to the public.

In 1949 further exploration revealed another chamber through which prehistoric men had entered the cave.

You can visit, though you are advised to telephone and reserve a place on a timed tour as the number of people passing through the seven halls, over a distance of a mile, is limited for safety reasons.

You will pass through an art gallery of mammoths, bison and horses, symbols, red or black punctuation marks, human figures, hand and foot prints. Petrified prehistoric footprints in wet clay, bones of cave bears and the roots of an oak tree which bore down to find moisture all are evidence of so much that has been kept hidden for thousands of years.

Travelling north through the National Park Region a short mention must be made of the village of Labastide Murat. It was founded in the 12th century by Fortanier de Gourdon, and known as La Bastide Fortanière. Later the name evolved into Fortunière. But it was in 1852 that it took the name of one of its famous citizens.

Joachim Murat, the son of the innkeeper in Fortunière, met Bonaparte in 1795 in Paris, a meeting which changed his life. He became *aide de camp* to Bonaparte, then General and soon married Napoléon's younger sister. His illustrious career continued with a promise of the title of Prince of the Empire and he later became King of Naples.

Thus the village, proud of Joachim Murat, adopted his name; the village from then on was known as Labastide-Murat. A museum set within the old inn tells you more of Murat's life.

Continuing farther north, through the National Park, but before you reach the border of the Dordogne and Lot Valleys, you will come to Gramat. Here the wild limestone plateau links the valleys of the Lot and Célé to the valley of the Dordogne. Yet more exciting sights await you here, including the Gouffre de Padirac.

~ *Gouffre de Padirac* ~

The most famous spectacle in this area is the Gouffre de Padirac, a chasm descending over one hundred metres to a subterranean river and lake.

Visitors reach the river by going down in a lift or walking down a long staircase. As you exit the lift you are ushered into a boat and gently paddled along 500 metres of the river to discover this underground world, arriving at a cavern named the *Lac de Pluie*, the Rain Lake. The journey then continues on foot through the vast galleries; the *Grands Cours* and on to the *Grand Dôme* with its ninety-four metre high arched roof. Here too is the *Lac Supérieur,* twenty-eight metres above the river bed! It's not an easy tour to undertake but if you have no fears of being deep underground, it is an amazing experience.

~ *Gramat* ~

Gramat is 'capital' of the area and has several fairs; sheep, nuts and truffles are the main attractions. Gramat is also famous for its Country Festival of concerts for amateurs. Rock, Rockabilly, Americana, Nashville sound, New Country and other Cajun Rock, all in honor of American culture. Exhibitions take place annually with parades of motor bikes and cars from across the Atlantic with shops selling Western products and, last but not least, dancing.

A little time to relax and unwind is on hand in *Les Jardins du Grand Couvent*. Behind the high walls of the convent of the Sisters of Our Lady of the Calvary, you will find a surprise. Amble along a kilometre of pathway and you will see colourful gardens, rose and flowerbeds, aromatic and medicinal plants, lavender and trees, with horses and donkeys in the meadow; there's an old wash-house and bread oven, exhibition rooms, a craft shop and importantly – a tea room!

Here too, just to the south of the village, is a 40 hectares park of animals in semi-captivity. You can visit the park and see these mainly European animals; wild horses, bears, wolves, bison, otters, pelicans, living in huge enclosures. There is also a botanical park.

~ *Rocamadour* ~

Travel north-west just a few miles for one of the most stunning sights of this area; Rocamadour. It is deemed to be the second most famous beauty spot in France, after Mont St Michel.

The construction of this mediaeval village, against the vertical rock face, defies belief, as it clings to the dizzying cliffs of the Alzou canyon. It is possible that the hermit Saint Amadour gave his name to Rocamadour but what is more credible is that it comes from the old language of the south of France, *langue d'Oc*, 'roc amator' which means rock lover, which in time became Rocamadour.

A 'Book of Miracles of Our Lady' from the 12th century, *le Livre des Miracles de Notre-Dame*, records that in 1166 a local man asked to be buried beneath the threshold of the Chapel of the Virgin. When the grave was dug they found  the body of a man which they placed near the altar. Soon miracles began to happen. The discovery of this incredibly preserved body was believed to be that of the hermit, Saint Amadour. Precious relics which the sanctuaries lacked, were thus provided, confirming Rocamadour's reputation as a special place of worship and pilgrimage. The origin of the veneration of the Virgin Mary in this village is unknown, but the Black Madonna with Jesus on her knee, placed above the altar in the chapel, is believed by experts to be from the 9th century.

It was a remarkable sanctuary and a centre of pilgrimage, an obligatory route for the pilgrims on the *Chemin de Saint Jacques de Compostelle.* The pilgrims had to climb the stone staircase to the sanctuary, 216 steps, some in chains, some on their knees! Their climb was rewarded with a certificate issued by the priest and the sight of the Black Madonna.

The pilgrims came to pray, to thank, to make atonement or to fulfil a wish. They left with their certificate and a *sportelle,* a badge evoking the scallop shell, the symbol of the *jacquet,* the Saint Jacque pilgrim. Made of lead, tin, gold or silver, it bore an effigy of Our Lady.

Many of the pilgrims had been ordered by an Ecclesiastical tribunal to make this journey and needed the certificate as proof that they had made the pilgrimage. Without it they were in danger, particularly the Albigensian 'heretics' who had escaped Simon de Montfort's crusade.

The Albigensians were members of a sect, who were originally called Cathars, a faith which it is thought to have had its origins in Eastern Europe. The name 'Cathars' is not one that they chose; they called themselves *Bons Hommes et Bonnes Femmes,* meaning Good Men and Good Women. The name Albigensian originated in the 12th century, and refers to the town of Albi (north east of Toulouse). The name is confusing as the movement flourished far and wide in the south of France, even in Italy, Germany, northern France, Belgium and Spain, and had no specific centre.

The Catharists or Albigensians were Christian but did not believe in the authority of either the Roman Catholic Church or the Pope. Some believed that the world was ruled by antagonistic forces of good and of evil. They strove for perfection in this life and looked for a world in which material things did not matter.

In 1208, after an unsuccessful campaign of conversion of the Albigensians by the Roman Catholic Church, the Pope's patience ran out. He ordered a Crusade against them, led by Simon de Montfort. Sieges and massacres resulted in thousands and thousands of cruel, brutal deaths.

In 1229 the war ended with the Treaty of Paris and the Inquisition was established to oust the remaining Albigensians. Over the decades some members of the sect, rather than face death, renounced their faith but never free from their past they were compelled to wear a yellow cross sewn onto their clothing. It took nearly a hundred years of persecution to eradicate the sect, during which time all their writings were destroyed.

Still a place of pilgrimage, Rocamadour is now an enchanting place to visit with many interesting facets; the remains of a former chateau and the hospital which housed the medieval pilgrims, the basilica of Saint Saviour, and the old village of 10th to 15th century houses, with streets and fortified gates which seem to retain the atmosphere of mediaeval times.

Near to Rocamadour are so many attractions it's difficult to decide which to visit. You'd need a long holiday to manage to see them all. There's such a diversity that all members of the family can find something to interest them.

~ *Grotte Prehistorique des Merveilles* ~

The 'wonders' of these caves, on the limestone plateau at Rocamadour, were discovered in October 1920. By the light of hollowed-stone lamps burning animal fat, men decorated this amazing cavern more than 20,000 years ago; outlined hands, horses and deer. This is not only art as it was at the time but is also a moving record of the spiritual life of the people, a mysterious merging of religion and art. Not as vast as *Pech Merle*, they are nevertheless of interest to the bold cave explorer.

~ *Forêt des Singes* ~

For those who prefer to stay above ground a visit to the *Forêt des Singes*, the Monkey Forest, will entertain and interest both adults and children. You can walk along paths through this 20 hectares park with an animal guide who tells you about the life and behaviour of these Barbary Macaques. As they peep through the leaves of the trees or even sit at the base of a tree, you have a close up view of their everyday lives. You can also help at feeding times.

A threatened species, originally from northern Africa, more than 130 of them live here in freedom. Several groups of monkeys born here in the park have been reintroduced into their original natural habitat.

~ *Rocher des Aigles* ~

If monkeys do not appeal to you, then a visit to Eagles Rock may be of interest. Open most of the year round there is a daily demonstration of eagles in flight. More than a hundred different varieties from all over the world, birds of prey and parrots with their unfurled wings provide hourly spectacles, the vultures sometimes soaring more than 1,000 metres into the sky. Returning to the ground with a signal from their trainers, they dive from the heights, an impressive sight.

~ *La capital de la Truffe* ~

In the southernmost tip of this region on the Causse de Limogne the truffle oak tree is king. The village of Lalbenque is known as the capital of the truffle. During the winter shopping baskets reveal their precious contents, the famous truffles, which are sold in the market on a Tuesday afternoon. At the end of the season, which runs from December to March, the final significant market of the Quercy region is held in Lalbenque.

Here in this village you can explore Saint Quirin church in gothic style with a baroque reredos of the 17th century. At the Porte du Ballat you'll find houses of corbelled construction and relics of the 100 Years War. Outside the village are numerous standing stones known as dolmens.

~ *Pays Bourian* ~

~ *Bourian Country* ~

In this western area bordering the department of the Dordogne, the earth is ochre and red, visible in the stone of the walled villages and the houses and in the earth itself. It's a complete contrast to the impressive landscape of the Causse; it's a land of trees, forests of oaks and sweet chestnut trees, of fern and heather. It's a quiet hidden land with hills and vales, meadows and streams. Cows graze peacefully in the flat fields of the valleys. Even the shape of the dark red roofs of houses is different; the gentle curve of the last third of an otherwise steep roof lends an enchantment to the form, reminding one of the gingerbread house in the fairy-tale Hansel and Gretel.

~ *Gourdon* ~

A most picturesque route driving north from Fumel will take you to Gourdon, the chief town of the Bourian country. A close neighbour is the area of Perigord, with whom the Bourian area shares similar tastes in good food and wine. The population of little above five hundred enjoys the tranquility and pleasure of living in this old market town.

It still has the ambiance of a Mediaeval town, with its fortified gateway and twisting, narrow streets, some no more than an alleyway. Its main street is a circle around the town where the ramparts used to be. To see some of the interesting details of the inner Mediaeval town, such as the Gothic pointed arches and half timbered houses in Majou Street where stood the shops and private apartments of the rich merchant families, you need to follow one of the designated walks. Two walks around the inner town are marked with arrows indicating Walk 1 or Walk 2, and a leaflet giving descriptions and explanations is available from the Tourist Office. Amongst other things, look for mullioned windows, a wrought iron staircase, and a dovecot. By the way, call in at the English bookshop just before the stone gateway, at the bottom of Majou Street. All books here are in English and you'll find some informative and interesting books on the area as well as good fiction reading.

Gourdon's most striking building is the 14th century church of Saint Pierre with its two great towers which can be seen from all directions. They dominate the village standing 35 metres tall, proudly overlooking the Saint Pierre square, and can be seen a long way out on the road to Fumel. Despite the cleaning and renovation of the stone of the 13th to 16th century, taking away something of their former charm, the old houses stand as witness to the past.

The castle and keep, which stood behind the church of Saint Pierre on a 284 metre high steep hill, were torn down by King Louis XIII to punish the local lord of the time. You can climb the many broad steps up to the top of the hill where there is now a stone table with an orientation map. Proudly, on the top of this hill flies the red flag bearing the Occitan cross.

During the Hundred Years War the Lords of Gourdon remained loyal to the French crown, unlike the neighbouring Périgord which went over to *les Anglais*, the fortress playing a part in protecting the Quercy region. According to a local legend, it is said that Bertrand, the Lord of Gourdon, was instrumental in causing the death of Richard the Lionheart at the siege of the *Château de Châlus-Charbol*, in the Limousin, in 1199.

Gourdon was at its peak in the 14th century, its prosperity due mostly to cloth making and weaving. As mentioned, the castle was razed to the ground by Louis XIII and the castle's fortifications destroyed in the 18th century but these were replaced by the present day boulevards.

Over the centuries pilgrims have passed through this village, the first stop after Rocamadour, on their journey to the shrine of Saint James of Compostela.

Gourdon is an ideal centre for visiting lovely mediaeval towns and villages in this area, each with its own history and interest.

Uzech-les-Oules is one such village where a pottery festival takes place every summer. In *langue d'oc,* the old Occitan language, 'oulo' means a cooking pot. In the Middle Ages there were many potters here because of the good clay, which is still available today. The every day cooking pots, which have been made for centuries, bear the distinctive traditional finial and glazing. Tradition continues but the potters of today are adapting designs to the needs and likes of the modern purchaser. It is said that 'art is second nature' in this area where artists and craftsmen have come over the centuries to fulfil their dreams.

Gourdon also has caves nearby, les Grottes de Cougnac. Though not as extensive as the caves of Pech Merle, they have remarkable prehistoric paintings of mammoths, ibex, human figures and various signs and symbols. These are the oldest representational drawings in France open to the public.

On the Fumel road going south, passing through the picturesque villages of Salviac and Cazals, you will come to the little village of Montcléra. Here on the roadside is a delightful castle. It is privately owned and not open to the public, but it's worth stopping the car just to quietly peer through the trees at what is a 15th century chateau in remarkable repair, but don't alarm the family dogs too much who will bark a reprimand for your nosiness! Hidden away also in this village is a completely restored Roman style 12th century church with three listed ornamental screens.

South of Gourdon in the village of Les Arques you'll find the fine Roman church of Saint Laurent with a former 12th century Benedictine priory; nearby frescoes in the 15th century chapel of Saint André; and Le Musée Zadkine.

Ossip Zadkine, a contemporary sculptor, was born in Russia in 1890 but lived most of his life in France. A lover of nature and trees he made frequent visits to the south west of France and in 1934 he chose to make his home here in Les Arques. It is said that the most important of his sculptures were created there. Though the museum contains only a limited number of his works, they are representative of his style and artistic talent. Three of his sculptures stand in front of the Saint Laurent church. It was Zadkine who discovered in 1954 the little roman chapel of Saint André, just a short distance from the village, where you will find the 15th century frescoes.

~ Pays de la Vallée de la Dordogne Lotoise ~

~ The Dordogne Valley in the Lot ~

The upper reaches of the river Dordogne flow through this the most northern section of the department of the Lot. Along this section of the Dordogne the banks were lined, long ago, with the landing stages of the former boatmen and their *gabarres*, the poled, flat-bottomed boats. The life of inland water transport lives on in today's boatmen offering gentle outings in river craft in which visitors may enjoy the amazing scenery.

In this fertile farmland you will find walnuts, the rather special delicate mushrooms the *cèpes,* and *la prune dorée,* the golden plum.

Here you will see a different shape of roof on the houses; they are steeply pitched so that they can take the weight of the *lauzes,* the flat stones, which are used instead of slates or tiles.

In this northernmost corner of the department of the Lot you will find no fewer than three of the *Plus Beaux Villages de France.*; Autoire, Loubressac and Carrenac.

~ *Autoire* ~

Autoire is a pretty village with awkward old streets, which, if you persevere, will lead you to a fountain in a small square, surrounded by half-timbered and old corbelled houses, with their white walls and red-brown roofs, and to grander houses with their pointed turrets.

In visiting this village first (before Loubressac, its neighbour) you will appreciate the quaint, somewhat higgledy-piggledy spread of houses with steep roofs, dormer windows and tall towers. The view from the terrace by the church reveals the amphitheatre of rocks which protect the village from the south west and a two kilometre walk from the centre of the village will lead you to a view of a 30 metres cascade, the sparkling water falling from this natural amphitheatre of white rocks.

~ *Loubressac* ~

The fortified village of Loubressac is in sharp contrast to Autoire, sitting on a rocky outcrop, reached by a long winding steep road. It is worth the climb; the impressive view overlooks the three valleys of the Dordogne, the Bave and the Célé, a tributary of the Dordogne. In his book *Les Delices de France*, 'Memories of a Trip', written in 1670, the traveller and writer Savinien d'Alquié wrote that this village 'is fit for a king'. Classed as a *Village Fleuri* with two 'flowers', it has narrow and sinuous streets lined with neat houses built of Quercy stone.

The red-brown 'tiles' and decorated balconies are a colourful sight; a chocolate-box picture.

~ *Carrenac* ~

Carrenac, a little to the north and almost on the border with the department of the Corrèze, actually lies on the banks of the river Dordogne and yet confusingly remains within the department of the Lot.

From early records of the 10th century there is reference to the municipality of Carrenac which later was handed over to the abbey of Cluny, which founded a priory there.

The beautiful cloisters of Saint Peter's church, half-Romanesque, half-Gothic, safeguard a sculpture of the late 15th century, a famous entombment in almost perfect condition, which rests in the Chapter Room. The church doorway has a beautifully carved tympanum.

On the outer wall of the château which stands beside and attached to the church of St Peter, is a bust of François Fénélon, a writer-priest. Just opposite Carrenac, in the middle of the river Dordogne, is the island of Calypso. Its name comes from 'The Adventures of Telemachus', written by Fénélon and published in 1699. It was for the royal student, Louis XIV's grandson the Duc de Bolurgogne, that he wrote the novel which became an immense success. These 'Adventures' are based on the Odyssey by the Greek poet Homer. The Odyssey tells the story of the wanderings of Odysseus, who was shipwrecked on the island where the nymph Calypso lived, and she fell in love with him. The island opposite the village of Carrenac is still named after Calypso.

Fénélon, following in his uncle's footsteps, became Dean of Carrenac.

Carrenac is also famous for its *prune dorée,* the golden plum. In the 16th century, the King, *François I*, received a gift of grafted plum trees from the ruler of Persia. The King gave them to the monks of Carennac priory who successfully cultivated them in what proved to be perfect conditions and climate. This sweet fruit, greenish gold in colour, was later named *Reine Claude*, after the King's first wife Queen Claude.

Travel upstream from Carrenac to St Céré which sits on the banks of the small river Bave. It's an ideal centre from which to tour this attractive countryside and visit the numerous charming and interesting villages.

St Céré is a delightful village with 12th century wooden houses, old streets, and a square – the *place du Mercadiel* – with its strong Mediaeval atmosphere, and the 15th and 16th century mansions.

In the 17th century St Céré became an important exchange centre for commerce which contributed to its development and prosperity. The charm of this village, and indeed its affluence, was noted by the writer Savinien d'Alquié in 1721, who seems to have been in the habit of making comments about places in this area, such as Loubressac mentioned earlier in this chapter. His remark says:

'In this little village everything makes for good food. It's a very fitting place for one's entertainment due to there being some pleasant folk, and other delightful benefits which one can enjoy.'

Surrounded by a series of castles St Céré escaped destruction and ruin from the various wars and is dominated by the two towers of the St Laurent chateau nearby. This château sits high on a hill and affords a stunning view across the countryside. A walk along the rugged path running round the castle gives a 360° view of the hills beyond with St Céré below. Here the artist, lithographer and ceramist Jean Lurçat lived from 1945 until his death aged 74 in 1966. This is where he designed richly coloured tapestries and is best known for revolutionizing the art of tapestry making. A museum is now housed in one of the towers, dedicated to and displaying his work.

His most famous works are in Angers, a town on the river Loire; a series of striking tapestries called 'Song of the World', depicting a modern view of life, the world and its possible ending.

Having discovered that the Lot is literally riddled with caves and potholer's dream, you will not be surprised to find that St Céré also has its own special *grottes*. No Paleolithic paintings here, the Grottes de Presque offer the cave explorer something different. In a series of chambers and galleries you will find numerous and strange rock formations in various colours. Some of the stalagmites are as tall as eight to ten metres high, some so slender they look like long thin candles. Though fascinating it isn't quite in the same league as the *Gouffre de Padirac* near Gramat in the Regional Natural Park of the Quercy Plateau.

Close by St Céré is the beautiful almost fairy-tale castle of Montal. The story behind its construction has a sad ending, unlike most fairy-tales where all's well that ends well.

It was built in 1534 by a widow named Jeanne de Balsac d'Entragues. It was a gift for her eldest son Robert, who was away fighting in Italy with Francis I. She spared no cost, appointing only the best builders, craftsmen, and artists. She had a high window built so that she could watch and wait for her son's return.

Only his body returned, sadly he was killed in the war. Jeanne was so distraught that she had the high window blocked up. Beneath it she had an engraver carve the words; 'Hope No More'.

During the Revolution the mansion became rundown and uninhabitable. In 1879 an asset-stripper bought the property but with the sole purpose of selling off all its treasures.

In some ways this story does have a happy ending because in 1908 a new owner, a patron Maurice Fenaille, bought what was left and restored the house. He tracked down from all over the world all the treasures and artistic pieces which he then bought at exaggerated prices. There was one item still missing, a stone doorway. Not to be defeated he commissioned the sculptor Rodin to make a replacement. Finally, when it was restored to its former glory he gave the Château de Montal to the nation in 1913. It is now open to the public all year round.

~ *Pays Quercy-Rouergue* ~

~ *Quercy Rouergue Country* ~

The area on the extreme east of the department of the Lot sits next to the departments of Aveyron on its south east corner, Cantal on its eastern side, and touches the Corrèze on the northern side. The river Lot forms the border with the Aveyron department, then crosses the boundary and continues to run eastwards almost as far as Decazeville. Just west of there the border has taken a turn to the north but the Lot ambles on eastwards for many a mile yet. It flows on right through the Aveyron and into the department of Lozère, in which it rises. The Rouergue has two distinct areas; the Ségala and the Limargue.

The Ségala is an area of steep granite hills and deep, narrow valleys; a rather wild and rugged countryside. The hills are all above 500 metres and some nearly 800 metres high at the Cantal border, which marks the beginning of the Massif Central. In this land the soil is acid, the climate damp; poor conditions for growing wheat. Instead rye, *seigle,* was grown here, which in the old Occitan language means rye, hence the name *Ségala.* The soil has been much improved by modern methods, and today you may see cattle grazing, the breeds of Limousin, the famous beef cattle, and Salers, with long horns and dark brown colour, which come from the Cantal region.

The Limargue, lying on the western side of the area, between the Causse de Gramat and the Ségala, is a fertile land, thanks to the river Célé, a tributary of the Lot, and the protective sandstone hills. Follow the river south west until you come to the Mediaeval town of Figeac. It's difficult to get away from these Mediaeval towns isn't it? Not that I would want to!

Figeac grew around a Benedictine abbey founded in the 9th century, by the King of Aquitaine, *Pépin* I. (The name makes me smile because it is sometimes used in a descriptive way meaning 'Pepin The Short'. The word *pépin* means 'pip' and I visualize a very small man!) The abbey was linked to that of Cluny and the small town was a stop on the route of St James of Compostela. The monks lured the peasants and skilled workers to work for them in the monastery and to work the land, providing for their agricultural needs. The town developed quickly from the 12th century onwards, due mainly to its position on the various interconnecting routes. Over the next two centuries the international trade grew and early records mention merchants from Figeac as far afield as northern Europe and south to the Mediterranean basin.

However, the plague and the Hundred Years War put paid to their prosperity and it was not until the 17th and 18th centuries that the town began to recover. Progressive destruction of the ramparts had opened up the town to the surrounding countryside. It was in the 19th century that an ambitious plan to restructure the town began but was only partially carried out due to a lack of money and to those who wished to preserve the architecture and the urban network of the past.

Figeac has now been thoughtfully restored due to a local politician, who later in his career became a minister, and made sure there was money enough to carry out the work.

There is much of interest; Renaissance half-timbered merchants' houses, with their distinctive drying galleries for flax and later tobacco, on the top floor; the *Hôtel de la Monnaie,* the Mint, and the two churches of Notre-Dame-du-Puy and Saint-Sauveur, you can be sure of seeing by following a guide map from the tourist office.

Here in Figeac is the museum *L'Ecriture du Monde,* The World of Writing, which is dedicated to the world's many different writing systems. The remarkable and gifted linguist Jean-François Champollion, born here in Figeac in the late 18th century, is famous for deciphering the hieroglyphics of the Egyptian text on the Rosetta stone. This museum was recently enlarged and restored, inside and out. On the outside are a thousand letters, symbols which tell that inside this museum is a world of writing to explore. The Champollion collection relates

how over 5,000 years ago, writing came to man. Some exhibits are interactive and carry the visitor all over the world and through the centuries.

North of Figeac are two Plus Beaux Villages de France; Lacapelle-Marival and Cardaillac.

The two villages are strongly linked through the powerful Cardaillac family. The charming 17th century castle, in Lacapelle-Marival, with its grey tiled, pointed roofed turrets like witches' hats, is a reminder of the family's wealth and power. It was erected beside the 13th century square keep, which has machiolations, that is openings in the upper floor of the watch towers, through which stones or burning objects could be dropped on attackers.

In nearby Cardaillac you can follow a guided tour through the old part of the village and see the house where wooden vats were made, the chestnut drying sheds, the prune steam room, the walnut oil press, the clog factory and a classroom of the beginning of the century. The cliffs around the village were natural fortifications incorporated into the ramparts and some parts of the 11th to 12th century towers, *Tour de l'Horloge* and *Tour de Sagnes,* are still evident.

Cajarc, an attractive village, lies on the very southern edge of this eastern region of the Lot. Its origins are lost in time but dolmen, standing stones, around the village, bear witness to the thought that it rose from Celtic times, and later Gallo-Roman influences, but like so many villages it suffered from frequent invasions and was almost lost. After some time fortifications were built and the village began to develop. During the Wars of Religion it became a Protestant

Protectorate. For more than a century it remained a Protestant stronghold until Cardinal Richelieu had the fortifications destroyed in January 1623. Some ruins remain; a fortified mill, old houses, the ramparts and a chapel for lepers.

In summer amongst other activities, an unusual fair takes place here in Cajarc; *La Foire à la Laine,* the wool fair. The sheep rearers from all around come to sell their weighed bundles of untreated wool, usually around the first week in August.

A surprising product from this area is saffron. It was produced in the Quercy region as early as the 13th century and was one of the principal riches of *Bas Quercy,* lower Quercy, up to the 17th century but disappeared from the scene of agriculture at the time of the Revolution.

In 1998 a group of saffron producers visited the area to discuss its reintroduction and it is today a viable enterprise. In October and November you can see the purple crocus flowers blooming once again on the limestone plateau.

The well-known French novelist Françoise Sagan was born in Cajarc in 1935, into a well-to-do family. The writing of her first novel, *Bonjour Tristesse,* at the age of 19, was an immediate bestseller and made her famous not only in France but also abroad. This story of a young girl's first love affair, as well as Françoise Sagan's later books, plays and screen writing have all been translated into many languages.

Françoice Sagan lived a somewhat self-indulgent life; 'I shall live badly if I do not write, and I shall write badly if I do not live,' she is known to have said. She had a weakness for fast cars, drinking and gambling. She married twice, both marriages ending in divorce, and suffered from ill health in later life. President Jacques Chirac said on her death in 2004, 'With her death, France loses one of its most brilliant and sensitive writers - an eminent figure of our literary life.'

About halfway between Cajarc and Montbrun, following the Lot, you will see a steep cliff overlooking a loop in the river, known as the *Saut de la Mounine*. The legend of the Mounine's Leap is a sorry story. It goes like this:

'Long ago, in the times of my grandfather's grandfather, the leader of a band of rogues plundered the Quercy region. This brigand captured the beautiful young daughter of a good family with whom he was in love, but who was promised to the son of a local Lord of Montbrun. Now, the brigand owned an intelligent female monkey which in the local Occitan language was known as *La Mounine*. Mounine, jealous of her master's love for the young girl whom he had imprisoned, decided to set the girl free and flee from her master with her. But the guards warned the brigand who with his men pursued them. There they were, driven back at the top of the peak of the steep cliffs between Cajarc and Montbrun, with no escape. Mounine, with malicious intent, hid the girl behind a bush but dressed herself in the girl's cloak, in order to confuse her master. She ran along the edge of the cliffs taunting the bandit and his men to seize her. But she jumped into the abyss, knowing that a monkey always falls on its feet. She was counting on her own litheness but unfortunately could not stop herself from falling over the cliff. From this day on, the brigand left the people of the region to live in peace. In memory of the brave monkey the spot was named *Saut de la Mounine*.'

This is a somewhat romanticised version of the story that I read elsewhere, which is much more cruel. Apparently in this other account, it is the Lord of Montbrun who ordered his daughter to be hurled from the cliff top, punishment for having a love affair with another Lord's son. A hermit who lived in the cliffs heard of the order and was so horrified by it that he intervened. He dressed a poor blind monkey in girls' clothes and flung it over the cliff edge. The Lord of Montbrun thought that he was witnessing the death of his daughter and immediately was full of remorse. To his relief he saw his daughter hiding against the cliffs and at once forgave her.

Whichever story you prefer, neither shows any regret for the demise of the monkey, even if in the first tale she is a spiteful creature.

~ *Within the Circle* ~

The small town of Montcuq has kept a mild flavour of its Mediaeval history in its narrow streets and corbelled houses. The 12th century square keep, 24 metres tall, which gives the town its distinctive silhouette, towers above the ancient houses in the streets around and below it, dominating the surrounding countryside. Long ago, in the 12th century the town was surrounded by ramparts. Of interest is the 14th century church of St Hilaire with its frescoes and octagonal bell tower, and the church of Saint Privat with a 17th century rood screen.

The Sunday market at Montcuq is a favourite with English visitors, though more and more often you will hear their voices intermingling with those of Dutch residents and visitors. The market stretches the length of the main street, which is on two levels, and continues  round the corner to the right, ending at a small crossroads. In the high season it is crowded, to put not too fine a point on it! A continuous procession of bargain hunters and souvenir seekers, gently push from one end to the other on the lower street level, making their way up the street to the right. Then everyone turns round and comes back, jostling along to make their way to the stalls on the upper street. Maybe on the way they will stop and have a coffee or beer at one of the two restaurants opposite one another in the middle of the village. By the way, if you feel like a little reading, pop into the English bookshop run by Sophie Bacou. It's a small shop crammed with books in English or French, new or secondhand.

The farmers' market in Montcuq is held on a Thursday morning and there you will find the good quality local produce; seasonal fruit and vegetables, poultry, cheeses, *foie gras*, honey, spices, patisseries and of course wine.

Many English people live in and around Montcuq so you will still hear the English voices out of season too. Zoe and Peter Scott, who you will read about later and run the holiday centre 'Mondounet', have lived just outside the village for twenty years.

Montcuq has an annual *Fête*, which is a grand affair. If you happen to be there at the right time there's much to do and see and you can join in the fun of the activities. Zoe and Peter Scott are always involved with its organisation and sometimes Peter sings at one of the concerts. The well-known French singer Nino Ferrer lived here for twenty years and in the past sang in the festival concerts. A picture of Montcuq en Quercy, which she painted in 1993 and then gave to the town, now hangs in the *Mairie*.

Another well-known event that takes place here is the annual sale of *Brocante*. The word 'brocante' covers a wide assortment of goods both in quality and age. Alongside a few genuine antiques there are goods that have, as are often described, come out of the attic. These events are fun to wander around and you never know you may be lucky enough to find a treasure, or at least pick up a bargain.

~ *Cahors Wine* ~

A last word on the department of the Lot must be given to *le vin de Cahors.*

Of course, vines are grown in the department other than in the Lot valley, for example on the southern border, known as the *Côteaux de Quercy,* but to qualify for the *Appelation d'origine Controlée de Cahors* they must be grown in a specific area; on both the north and the south alluvial terraces of the river Lot, and on the chalky plateau, from Puy-l'Evêque near the border with Lot-et-Garonne at the western end, reaching over thirty kilometres eastwards as far as Cahors.

Tempered by its distance from the coast and its proximity to the Massif Centrale, the climate is gentle and humid. This east-west orientation gives rise to a channel through which the west winds blow and sweep the plateau. On the other hand when the north-west or south winds are dominant, there is a gentle warming effect.

The principal grape is the Malbec, sometimes called the Auxerrois or Côt, names which did nothing but confuse me when I first became acquainted with Cahors wine. At one time Cahors wine was not considered amongst the best. A friend of mine once described it as 'black ink' and at the time I took his word for it. However, its quality has definitely been raised over the last few years to the level of *grands crus,* a wine of good vintage.

You are spoilt for choice when it comes to a *dégustation,* the vineyards along the route welcome you. It's a wine to be drunk with the traditional recipes of the south west; *confits de canard* and *magret de canard,* duck leg and duck breast; *foie gras;* Quercy lamb and early vegetables to be found in the markets in the spring.

If you start near Tournon d'Agenais, along the D656 and travel for only a few kilometres you will come to Saux. You can call in on François Alleman for a dégustation, or travel along a little farther and you will see the sign to Le Boulvé, where Didier Ibre produces wine. Read their stories later in this section.

You will also see on this route an enormous mock wine bottle, boldly advertising the *Vin du Tsar*, bearing a picture of Nicolas II of Russia. It makes us smile every time we pass by as our very young grand daughter was heard to whisper to her sister,

'Wow, what a huge bottle! Mummy would be tipsy if she drank that!' What intrigued me about it was what could possibly be the connection with the Tsar.

Over a period of time the wine from this vineyard at Thézac had become well known, and appealed to, amongst others, the famous Napoleon III and President Fallière, President of France from 1906 to 1913.

It was President Fallière, an ardent promoter of local wine and gastronomy, who served the wine to the Tsar, who was at that time a guest of his. The Tsar was impressed and immediately issued a commendation. This spread through the vineyard where the wine he had so enjoyed was produced. Over the years it became known as the wine that the Tsar had chosen, the wine that he wanted, and so it became known as *Vin du Tsar*.

Now comes the surprise. It is not strictly a Cahors wine! Why? Because the vineyard is just outside the department boundary, it lies in fact in the *Lot et Garonne*. But don't let that deter you from a *dégustation*.

Read now the stories of some of the interesting people I have met in this corner of the Lot, two of whom are the *vignerons,* wine makers of Cahors wine, mentioned above.

Francis Alleman

Vigneron

Farmer, vine grower and wine producer

Francis Alleman is a gentle, smiling man whose bronzed face is evidence of an outdoor life. Despite his lean build one can see he is strong. He is the fourth generation to own and work on this *domaine*.

It was his great grandfather who bought the *exploitation,* the plot of land, which began what is now an 85 hectares (180 acres) property, known as Le Domaine des Boulbènes. It is divided into a 15 hectares vineyard and a 70 hectares farm.

The land of his great grandfather passed to his son Leonce Germain, and then to his two daughters – Angèle and Jacqueline. Sadly Jacqueline died very young and so Angèle, Francis' mother, inherited Le Domaine de Boulbènes.

Francis now runs the 15 hectares vineyard almost single-handedly. Though the grapes are gathered by machine, workers do come in at the time of the *vendange,* the grape harvest, to sort them by hand. Francis' only other co-worker is his eighty two year old father who helps farm the 70 hectares of land, growing grain and cereal crops. Their work is endless and, as with all nature, unremitting. Francis and his family manage to take a short break from time to time but they never have a prolonged 'holiday'. The land won't wait for its master and Francis is dedicated to his vision; that of producing good wine.

'There have always been vines here in this area, for centuries,' he says. And we begin to talk about the *cépages,* the grape variety, which he has planted here at Le Domaine des Boulbènes.

'Originally the grape variety was Jurançon, which was producing rather a rough Cahors wine and they were old vines,' he says.

'The wine was sold to *negociants, en vrac* in the old days,' that is sold in bulk to wine merchants. 'Now we bottle our own here – *élevé et mise en bouteilles sur la propriété,*' he says with a proud smile. To grow the vines, harvest and make the wine, and bottle it on the estate, is something to be justly proud of.

And so in 1981 he began the replanting of the *vignoble,* the vineyard.

'I started with the grape varieties Auxerrois and Merlot to produce *vin de Cahors.*' Auxerrois is the Cahors name for the Malbec grape.

It was in 2002, he continues, that he planted the Cabernet Sauvignon and Cabernet Franc, and Gamay for his *vin du pays,* and then more Merlot followed.

'We are making better wine now, in fact we are making good wine,' he says honestly but without bragging.

It's true; the prizes prove it.

In 2004 he planted Chardonnay, in a small area of his property called Bourlens. This was the cause of some excitement in the department of the Lot, especially as Bourlens is just across the department boundary and nestles in the Lot et Garonne. It seemed that local people were a little anxious about this bold and innovative move of his. Planting a white wine grape in an area generally regarded as producing red wine, and in particular the Chardonnay grape, provoked a few raised eyebrows. The choice of Sauvignon or Semillon which are generally planted in the nearby Bordeaux area, might have been less of a surprise.

Francis produced his first rosé wine in 2004 - Cabernet Sauvignon and Auxerrois mixed - a very nice wine. But he wasn't satisfied. He cares deeply about the quality of his wine and thought he could do better; produce a finer wine from Cabernet Sauvignon only. He consulted his *oenologue* – his wine adviser, with whom he works very closely, and whom Francis says is 'brilliant'. Francis generously lays the success of the *rosé* at his door. The result of their collaboration was a beautiful, pale rosé, with a hint of orange, which took 1st Prize, out of sixty submitted, in the Rosé Section of the *Vins de Pays du Lot* Wine Fair.

In 2005 came his triumph with red wine. In the 'Value for Money' section (that is quality and price) in the June 2006 French Wine Review, his *Rubis de Roche* received just recognition. Out of ten thousand bottles submitted only 1,200 are selected; *Rubis de Roche* came second out of the 1,200.

In the section Ten of the Great Successes, his Domaine des Boulbènes, with a 70/30 blend of two grape varieties, he gained the award of Two Glasses; the symbol used in the wine world equivalent to stars given to chefs and restaurants, and he came second out of the ten in the Two-Glass category.

All of this is an extraordinary achievement for what is, in effect, a one man band and a relatively small independent *vigneron*, honouring the Charter of Independent Wine Makers.

The first vendange of Chardonnay was in 2006 and if recent record is anything to go by there will be some good Chardonnay white wine available soon from Francis' special vineyard.

A local event in the village of Saux, right next to where his property is situated, is the annual Wine Fair held in July, where several neighbouring *vignerons* take a stand offering their wines for a *dégustation*, a

free tasting. You will find Francis there, softly smiling, offering his wines for a tasting, along with relevant information on their production.

The Fair is an event in itself. The opening is heralded by a noisy but rhythmic, musically exciting band led by a rotund, expert drum player who performs amazing acrobatic manoeuvres with his huge drum, whilst maintaining a strong musical hold on his musicians. They perform throughout the evening, entertaining the guests who enjoy, alongside the wine, a variety of regional foods and in particular a barbecued supper of duck and flavoursome duck sausages, a local speciality.

Francis Alleman does not sell his wine in the markets. He has a reputation locally and a loyal clientelle, also selling to a well known Brasserie in Brussels.

It's not surprising that he is successful; he is dedicated to making good wine and works hard to that end.

Behind this story of success through commitment and hard work, lies another story; one of romance and sadness. It begins with Marie, Francis' paternal grandmother, from whom, through his father, he inherited the domaine at Bourlens.

Young Marie was an heiress; a plot of land of just four hectares came to her on her father's death. There was a small house on this land too, but it was in bad repair, falling down around her.

Then into Marie's young life came a penniless young man, walking onto the land with nothing but his great boots in his hands. The two fell in love and married. He was small in height, Marie was tiny and slender. They worked together and were happy, having two children, Marius and Etienne. Suddenly Marie's husband died. How was Marie to work these four hectares of land, alone, and provide for her children? It was not possible.

Marie had no choice but to move with her two children. She was offered a room in a relative's cottage in the village, at least here she was not alone. She toiled on other people's land to scrape a living, sometimes having to walk for miles to reach her work; during which time she watched her house fall slowly into disrepair and finally tumble down. But the one thing she would not do was sell her four hectare plot of land. She was cajoled, coerced, even bullied, but she would not sell.

In due course Marie's elder son, Marius, took over the land at Bourlens. He never married and with no children of his own promised that eventually Marie's grandson Francis should inherit the land. In fact, on Marius' early death, the land first passed to his own younger brother Etienne, before passing to Francis.

Marie shared her birthday date, the 6th of January, with her grandson Francis,and lived until she was 93 years old. If she could but see this four hectare area of land now, that she so bravely hung on to, she would be proud. This is where Francis has planted his Chardonnay.

Bourlens is in the Lot and Garonne, just the other side of the border of the Lot. The bureaucratic separateness of the departments in France is a fact, sometimes experienced in the most trivial of ways. Here the official line dividing the Lot et Garonne and the neighbouring Lot, is invisible, yet Le Domaine des Boulbènes transcends the boundary, a melding of the land in the two departments.

In 1999 Francis launched into a new venture. He started a plantation of oak trees, *des chênes aux truffiers*. Truffles! Around the base of the oak trees the truffles form. There seems to be no holding Francis – one wonders how he manages to cope with the work load and what he will come up with next! But he is happy on the land and thrives on his success through commitment and resolve.

Francis and his wife, Josette, have two children Daniel and Christian.

'Will they carry on the family tradition of winemaking?' I asked Francis.

'Who knows? Perhaps.' He shrugs. 'Maybe they'll go off and do something else for a while and then come back again. That's possible.'

Perhaps the young boys are already aware of the necessary dedication and commitment to the land and are not yet ready to make that promise. As Francis says, '*On verra*' – we'll have to wait and see. Josette leaves the winemaking to Francis – she is happy in her job as secretary to the *Maire*.

One can visit the *caves* every day from 9am to 12 noon and 3pm to 7pm. Quite often Francis, down to earth and natural, will arrive from the fields on his tractor to say hello to his customers. Until recently, Kate Coleridge, an English friend of Francis', used to come to the *caves* to help during the summer months of July and August. She would be on hand to guide the non-French speakers with their wine tasting.

Kate, a direct descendent of the famous poet Samuel Taylor Coleridge, also writes poetry in both English and French. Her poem of the story of Marie is reproduced here, with her kind permission.

207

MARIE DE BOURLENS

Je suis venue te chercher, Marie,
Pour essayer de trouver ta maison:
Mais il n'en reste rien, même pas une pierre.
Quand-même, Marie; c'est glorieux,
Cette vue que tu as :
Ce n'etait pas pour rien que tu as gardé ta terre.
Mais la nature est indifférente à la peine
Et les hiver peuvent être froids.

Je suis venue ce matin, Marie,
Et j'ai pensé à ton histoire.
Quand la cloche a tinté, tu es tombé à genoux
Et ce n'était pas pour prier.
Tes jambes s'écroulaient au cimetière
A côtè du cercueil où ils ont mit ton mari.

Veuve si jeune, ma pauvre et fière,
Avec tes enfants, leurs yeux ronds et effrayés,
Qui empoignaient ta robe!
Tes larmes n'étaient pas pour rien, Marie,
Mais tu ne pouvais pas le faire revenir
Porté sur la marée de ton chagrin.
Ils sont venus quand, Marie,
Avec leurs langues épaisses d'avarice,
Tous ces voisins, ces amis, ces fantoches
Avant qu'il fallut quitter ta maison
Pour une chambre dans le village
Le chuchotement commençait
        ~~ une brise à travers les volets.

Elle doit vendre sa terre,
Elle doit vendre
Elle doit.....

Voilà, Marie, j'en ai de l'or.
C'est caché dans ma serre-
Vends-moi ta terre!
Et voilà, Marie, mon argent
Est trop lourd pour mes poches
Vends-moi ta terre!
Tu as craché sur leurs pieds,
Tu as fait claquer la porte,
Tu n'as pas vendu
Et ce n'était pas pour rien.

Les ronces se sont glissées par ton escalier;
Comme des voleurs elles ont cassé tes fenêtres.
Est-ce que tu as vu cette dégringolade
Quand tu es passé pour travailler dans les champs des autres,
Tes mains à vif sur la houe?
Mais, tu vois, Marie, ce n'était pas pour rien:
Ton fils et son fils ont fait
La renaissance de ta terre.
Ils l'ont fait avec fierté et soin.
C'est bien-aimé, ton Bourlens.

Et moi qui suis venue, par hasard, l'étrangère,
Je m'allonge sur ton sol ensablé,
Au repos sous le soleil
Parmi les petites vignes, leurs vrilles
Agrippées comme les doigts d'un nouveau-né.

Kate Coleridge, October 2005.

Zoe and Peter Scott

Vacances en compagne

Holiday centre in the countryside

Twenty years ago Zoe and Peter Scott settled in the department of the Lot, on the edge of the captivating mediaeval village of Montcuq. How they came to buy their 17th century Quercy farmhouse Mondounet is a story in itself but from the moment of their arrival they were determined to integrate into this French community. Now they are so involved in the life of the village, speaking fluent French, that one would think they had lived here all their lives. Even so, they have retained their pleasant Englishness, and Peter his wacky sense of humour!

Peter left behind a job as General Manager in a Timber Preservation Company, Zoe a job in Advertising and Marketing, in Portsmouth, to take up life with their ten year old daughter Nicola, in a tumble down farmhouse. Peter spoke no French, Zoe had what she remembered from school, so along with Nicola they embarked on some private tuition. They didn't have long to learn, it was a matter of months from the moment they paid their deposit on the property, in the September of that year, to the moment they unpacked their goods and chattels in their new home in February of the following year. Within a short space of time they had settled into the farmhouse, the only habitable building on the property, and renovated one of the other buildings into delightful self-catering accommodation. In May they were welcoming guests. What a year!

One of their first tasks, on arrival, was to find a school for ten year old Nicola. It was the tiny school in the nearby village of Belmontet with only thirteen pupils, aged 6 to 10, who were taught in small groups by one teacher. This is where Nicola began to learn a completely different method in Mathematics, learn French history, and of course begin to learn the French language. Speaking very little French at first, she was a novelty, but as a gregarious and spirited child she made herself understood with smiles and body language.

~ Nicola's Story ~

It was at school that Nicola found she had to change her name; the English pronunciation of the name Nicola is the same as the French pronunciation of the boy's name Nicolas (the 's' is silent) and so she became Nicole. During her first year in France Nicola went on a skiing trip to the Pyrénées; the family were keen skiers and she was accustomed to the sport. With no opportunity to speak English during the course of that week, Nicola returned speaking much better French, sadly she also returned with her leg in plaster; having injured her knee in a fall. It was to prove to be a problem for several years; physical activity so easily strained the knee and she needed to use crutches from time to time until surgery, first in a hospital in *Cahors* and later in *Lyon*, finally alleviated the problem when she was seventeen years old.

Zoe had realised what a difficult time Nicola would have adjusting to a new life and a different language. Both she and Peter were concerned about her education and how quickly she would be able to pick up the French language. But they needn't have worried; it happened all of a sudden.

Zoe and a local French friend had decided to go for a walk and Nicola trundled along despite the fact that she had a sore throat and had almost completely lost her voice. Suddenly Nicola joined in the conversation - in French! Her voice was croaky but she spoke and the French came tumbling out. From then on there was no holding her back.

It was on another skiing holiday in the Alps that Nicola made a friend who lived in Lyon. The following summer she visited her and there she met Lionel. They were only sixteen years old but they fell in love. Very soon Nicole decided that when she went to university it would have to be in Lyon; it was a good university of course, but Lionel would be there! The time came to apply for a place and with determination and planning she applied for a grant and found herself a flat there for the duration of her studies. After reading for an English degree Nicola spent a year in Paris gaining a qualification in translating. It was some eight years later, after Nicola had finished her studies, that she and Lionel married. They visit Montcuq whenever they can, along with their three year old son Thomas, who of course is growing up bilingual. Nicola continues to work for a large chemical company, she liaises between the company in Lyon and the English companies, using her bilingual skills.

~ *Mondounet* ~

Much of the renovation and building work on the property of Mondounet has been done by Peter, with help from local labour and a French mason. A mason in France is an '*artisan*', which is a recognised and respected vocation, he is often an imaginative and resourceful fellow, much more than a 'builder'.

With his previous DIY skills and a battery of books (in French of course) Peter learned not only the terminology but the know-how to transform what looked like an impossible building task into an attractive group of dwellings. Zoe, with her more advanced French, did the sourcing and ordering of materials, and kept track of the mountains of paperwork!

Zoe and Peter's carefully restored buildings now offer self-catering accommodation in what were once upon a time the Barn, the Stable, and the Bread Oven! But don't expect to see the farm animals sharing your lodgings, or to smell the aroma of baking bread, for these charming holiday homes are beautifully appointed whilst retaining the character and the essence of their former use.

Each independent property is a self catering home with all facilities and its own private garden. But Peter hasn't finished. The mammoth task he undertook some years ago of restoring the buildings as holiday homes is more or less complete, but he and his mason are still renovating and improving the property in various ways.

The heated, shared swimming pool is enormous, fenced now to comply with the recent French safety laws. A delightful cabin, with services, provides a good spot for a cooling drink or a snack. Beside it is the barbecue where Peter cooks once a week for all the clients, who pay a nominal sum for a delicious meal.

Peter loves cooking and he and Zoe cook meals together. Peter professes to have no talent, he says he just follows the wonderful recipes from up-to-the minute cookery books, there's always one to be seen on the bookstand in their kitchen in the farmhouse; when I visited this week it was Rick Stein's 'Odyssey'.

~ *Life in Montcuq* ~

Zoe and Peter's first year was demanding but they didn't wait until they had time to get to know their village and to mingle with their neighbours. Within that first year they were involved in the celebrations for the 200th anniversary of the 1789 French Revolution. Both Zoe and Nicola were in the *son et lumiere* show, a re-enactment of the Storming of the Bastille. It was produced by Françoise Lowinsky, a renowned Parisienne dance teacher and choreographer, along with professional technicians – colleagues of hers who gave their time freely – to create a top quality spectacle. Only the players were amateurs, all local people. The then famous sixties singer Nino Ferrer, sadly now dead, sang the finale – the Marseillaise of course, and along with the whole cast, Zoe, Peter and Nicola joined in.

These days both Zoe and Peter are on several different committees in Montcuq. Zoe is a Vice President of the Association of Montcuq – *Loisirs Amicales Montaquois*, known as LAM. Zoe became involved with LAM when she joined their dance class, when they first arrived in Montcuq. Classes in patchwork and other leisure pursuits are held in the *Salle des Fetes* in Montcuq, the village hall is a very important meeting place in all French villages. Peter is a Vice President of the *Comité de Jumelage*; concerned with the twinning of the town of Cinigiano in Tuscany, Italy. They are also on the committee of '*Cours et Granges*' which organises a music festival, usually in July, sometimes taking place in different villages, such as Montcuq, Puy-l'Eveque, and

Le Boulvé. A recent concert in Montcuq was held at Chateau Janés where a barbecue and a caberet were popular events, Peter cooked the barbecue of course!

July is certainly the festival month in and around Montcuq. Look out for *Montcuq en Scène,* one spectacle after another packed into a weekend – and you are sure to meet Peter or Zoe somewhere.

As if all these activities and involvement were not enough, they both have hobbies. Peter plays table tennis and sings, sometimes in French, in a Blues-Jazz-Rock and Roll group. Zoe teaches dancing and keep fit. And of course, don't forget the cooking. Peter is very inventive and happily shares his popular barbecue recipe. Look for it at the end of this chapter.

Zoe recalls how when they first came to this area there were very few English people living here, or even visiting on holiday. For the last twelve years she has worked for a local estate agent *Quercy Gascogne Immobilier* and has met many English people wanting to buy in the area. She generally works from home; going into the office to see clients, taking them to view properties, carries out searches with other agencies, helps purchasers through the sales from negotiating the price to signing the completion documents. She has her own website which deals with holiday bookings at Mondounet but also for finding properties for people who want a holiday home or a permanent residence. Of course, would be purchasers can benefit from the delightful accommodation – either bed and breakfast or self-catering – whilst they explore the surrounding countryside.

So do Zoe and Peter ever relax one wonders? Of course they go to Lyon to visit Nicola, Lionel and Thomas and they visit friends, and Zoe's mother in England. They go skiing in the Pyrénées and the Alps with both English and French friends, sometimes making up a party, anything from six to twenty-six. And who organises it? Peter of course!

Here is something Peter offers his holiday makers on one of the special evenings.

'This recipe, if you can call it that, is so simple and easy to prepare and cook. The barbecue does it for you!' he says.

Marinated Prawns and Scallops

Method
Marinate prawns and scallops in lemon juice for half an hour.

Wrap each prawn and scallop in flattened rindless streaky bacon, held together with a cocktail stick.

Grill on the barbecue for a few minutes on each side.

Serve with lemon wedges and a mixed salad.

Sizzlingly delicious!

I cannot end the story of Zoe, Peter and Nicola, without telling you that Nicola and her husband now have a daughter, Lucille, to keep her brother Thomas company!

Didier and Josiane Ibre

Viticulteur

Wine grower and wine producer

Didier Ibre and his family came from Agen, where Didier worked as a wine representative for a large wine merchant.

It was his parents' purchase of a house in Grézels, as a holiday home in the department of the Lot, which, in time, brought about a radical change in Didier's career.

The house though in a poor state of repair, did not deter Didier's parents from buying the property. The surrounding open countryside was picturesque, a welcome contrast to their home in Agen. The Grézelois hills were a place for their children to roam free in the holidays, and enjoy the fresh air; four hectares of peace and calm. Looking at the state of the old house and all it would entail to renovate it, Didier's parents decided to build themselves a new house, set to one side some 300 metres from the semi-ruin. Little did they imagine that one day this semi-ruin would be a house their son and family would be proud of.

It was in 1981 that Didier and his wife Josiane, took the courageous step of breaking away to begin the creation of their own vineyard on those four hectares, on the Grézelois slopes. Not only did they have the planting of a vineyard to accomplish  but also the renovation of that tumble-down house, in which to accommodate the family of three children.

Looking out at the rows of vines, Didier frowns slightly and tells me,

'I don't come from a wine making background, you know. My father was a photographer and my mother worked in a hospital. And even though I had worked in the wine business it was quite a serious leap for me to start from scratch, knowing that I had a family to support.'

So Didier is not a long established *vigneron,* 25 years in the wine making business is not considered long, but he has built up his business slowly and surely, and is proud to be the proprietor of Le Pech d'Estournel. Didier claims this *domaine* has a scent of the land all its own, and his publicity flyer showing how to find the vineyard, poetically describes it as '*un parfum de terroir et d'authenticité,* the authentic scent of the land.

'It's very supportive, having a family who are ready to lend a hand on the *vignoble*,' he says. He is talking of his three children; Aurelien, the eldest, is now twenty-five and is a *charpentier,* a fine woodworker. Sarah, the youngest at 20, is studying to be a primary school teacher, but it is Laetitia the 24 year elder daughter, who has made wine making her career.

Laetitia has completed the *Brevet Professionel Vigne et Vin,* passing her exams to achieve the Diploma in professional winemaking. Laetitia recently became engaged to Jorge, who comes from Argentina. The same type of grape, the Malbec, which is planted on the family Ibre's vineyard, is grown in Argentina. Jorge is one of only three young people who won a place to come to France for some training. For three consecutive years, for a period of three months each year, he worked at Pech d'Estournel. With Laetitia's knowledge and growing expertise they will make a fine partnership in the winemaking business in Argentina. Of course Didier and Josiane were delighted to announce their daughter's engagement in July, to marry in April 2007, but it was tinged with a little sadness, knowing that Laetitia will be returning to Argentina with Jorge. 'We'll just have to go and visit them,' Didier says bravely.

Josiane who speaks a little English, is as much involved in the business as her husband, taking care of the accounts and the administration – 'a lot of paper work' she tells me with feeling.

'I also sell the wine, here in our home, when people come for a *dégustation.* I really enjoy the wine tasting sessions, singing its praises of course, and listening to peoples' comments. And I also attend the exhibitions. So, yes, in answer to your question, I *am* involved in the business, and I like it that way.'

In order to create his vineyard, Didier had to tear out a wood on this small plot, on ground of clay, chalk and stones! 'Plenty of stones,' he says with a rueful grin. He began by planting one hectare at a time, making improvements as he went along. He planted Malbec vines, which he tells me is typical for Cahors wine; and then some Merlot.

His wine carries the *Appelation Controlée* of Cahors and this small vineyard produces about 20,000 bottles of red, 1,000 bottles of rosé and 2,000 bottles of white wine, per year. The rosé is *le rosé de saignée,* which means that the grapes are put in the wine vat and the juice taken off, without pressing.

Josiane says enthusiastically,

'Our red *vin de Cahors* is just right to accompany a *cassoulet, confit de canard* or a *coq au vin de Cahors.'* So try it with duck, Toulouse sausages or chicken.

Didier prefers to hand pick the grapes, which he feels is a kinder way of harvesting them, and 'It makes them easier to sort' he says. 'I'm very strict about taking out the dry or mouldy ones' he emphasises.

He is proud to say that his wine is made on the premises, thus he is classed as a *Vigneron Independent,* adhering to the Charter of Independent Winemakers. None of his wine goes to a co-operative.

In the last few years Didier has made some adjustments to his wine making, due to changes in the weather.

'We have had some hot very dry summers in the recent past. Unlike the years 1984 to 1987 which were very wet. In the warmer weather the sugar forms naturally and so I have not needed to add sugar.' Then he speaks of the law in France, against watering the vines. 'In order to maintain quality, unlike new world production, I can only water in a heat wave!'

You can visit Didier's *vignoble* for a *dégustation*; they are open from 9am to 12 noon, and 2 pm to 6-30pm, and of course you may buy the wine on the premises. His wine is also for sale at several markets in the area. Laetitia, with an attractive smile, and knowledge of the wines, used to preside over their modest stall at Montaigu de Quercy on Saturdays, Montcuq on Sundays, Pressac on Fridays and Puy l'Eveque on Tuesdays, but now Sarah has taken over.

My favourite, for summer drinking, is their light rosé - *Vin de Pays du Lot*, at a very reasonable price. Didier sells to restaurants and often, through them, clients come to buy his wine, having drunk it at the restaurant.

If he could, Didier would have liked to increase the size of his vineyard but he no longer has the right to purchase more land. And, by law, he is not allowed to plant more vines.

'If I wish to plant vines in a different place on my land, then I am obliged to tear out some existing vines. I have four and a half hectares and I'm not allowed to have more. The only right I have is to replant, having first scrubbed out the same number of vines elsewhere on the vineyard.

I ask Didier if neighbouring *vignerons* ever help each other.

'Oh no,' he says unequivocally. 'A *vigneron's* life is demanding and there isn't time to spare to lend a hand elsewhere.'

Certainly the Ibre family don't have much spare time. The renovation of their house and outbuildings is still going on. Didier is particular about the quality of his work and it's obvious he is making an excellent job of some stonework. I tease him, saying;

'If you ever get tired of being a *vigneron* you can always offer your services as a mason.' He shakes his head;

'I'll never get tired of making wine!' is his response.

In October and in February Didier travels to Paris to promote his wine at the wine exhibitions, taking a stand in *Le Salon du Livre Ancien*, where the exhibitions are held. Although this means leaving the *vignoble* for a short period of time it's not a holiday.

Even so, the Ibre family manages to take a holiday in the winter. When the *vendange* is over and the year's wine made, any time between December and February, then they can escape. It's usually to the sun; a favourite destination being Egypt. December to February is an ideal time for skiing, which Didier would like to do, but Josiane doesn't like it, so...

'It's out of the question,' Didier says with a sigh and adds, 'After all, she works hard too, and deserves a holiday.'

Since first talking to Josiane and Didier Ibre, Lataetitia has married Jorge. They are now living in Argentina.

Marc and Françoise Laugier

Fromage de Chèvre

Goat's Cheese

It's the first of March, a cold, windy day with just a glimmer of sun, which after a week of pouring rain is a cheering presence. I'm driving along narrow, winding roads, up the side of the ridge, through plantations of vines, one after the other, and I wonder at the black silhouettes of leafless vines, looking as though they will never come to anything; but they have plenty of time, once the land warms up they grow rapidly. As I reach the top, the view is extensive, right and to left and in front of me, I feel as though I am on top of the world. In fact it's not very high at all, as I learn later from Marc when I arrive at the *fromagerie.*

There's not a soul in sight and I dread meeting a car coming in the other direction. This road is so narrow there's absolutely no chance of passing another vehicle; the bank rises to my right and there is a considerable drop to my left.

But I do see a solitary figure, clad in wind-cheater; he's pruning those unpromising looking vines, down to their one waving twig.

I drive beyond the vines into a vista of oak trees, their bark equally black as those dormant vines. As the pale sun catches the greeny-silver lichen which spreads over the trunks and branches of the trees, it gives them an eerie look. Amongst them are juniper trees. The hillside slopes down into the valley, to the river Lot below where you will find chestnut trees. On the northern side of the river is Puy l'Eveque glistening white in the afternoon sun.

I've twisted and turned so many times through this wild bleak landscape, I'm apprehensive about finding my way back home.

But Marc will give me directions I'm sure.

And it is for Marc and Françoise Laugier's goat farm, La Gard'Haute, that I am aiming. Down a last unmade track and I am here. They give me a warm welcome; Marc still wearing his white protective coat and hat, and his white clogs, having come straight from his cheese dairy.

What a view they have from their house, perched on the hillside, the land dropping down to the river Lot in the distance.

La Gard'Haute poised above the Lot valley, dominating Duravel, Vire sur Lot and Grézels, was formerly a tiny village. At one time forty people lived here making their living as *vignerons*. The arrival of phylloxera in 1880 destroyed the vines, the people drifted away; the last inhabitant left in 1940.

I am standing with Marc admiring the view as he tells me how his *fromagerie* began.

In 1960 his parents, originally from the centre of France, near Tours in la Tourraine, where Marc was born, decided to move to the department of the Lot. They bought La Gard'Haute and the land, which over the intervening twenty years had become wild.

'We rescued it,' Marc says. 'We set about clearing the land and opening it up. We repaired an old house and later rebuilt the sheepfold. It was the sheep and goats which helped to clear the fields of brushwood. Farming and the rearing of sheep and goats were returned to the land.'

Then Marc left home and set off on his career. He travelled the world for some years, working in industry; in minerals and petrol, and in nuclear submarines, all in different countries. It wasn't until 1983 that he came back to France and decided to leave his profession.

'Following an obviously successful career, that was a brave decision,' I say to Marc. 'It's quite a leap to come from an industrial background into farming.'

'Yes true, but I've always loved the land and working with nature. My parents were not farmers but everybody in those days had a few animals and my mother knew how to make cheese, so I came into it fairly naturally. I needed a change back then and remember, I knew this place and was certain of the fact that I could live and work here. I've always felt the pull of the land – it gives me so much. People who work in the towns don't see the seasons changing or feel the rhythm of life; I know, from my previous career. Cheese-making is a very good profession, it's working entirely with nature. But it is hard work; seven days a week, every day of the year. There are no holidays and no sick pay! If you want to do it then the land will give something to you, but you need to love it – and I do!'

Françoise came originally from Normandy, and later worked in education in Paris, with under-privileged children.

'I had a house in this area and when visiting on one occasion some friends introduced me to Marc. We were married soon after. By this time Marc had started his *fromagerie.* He already had eighteen goats. Then together we decided to continue the restoration of La Gard'Haute, bringing in water and electricity, being careful to preserve the natural setting. We continued to rear goats and then built the cheese dairy. We began with *crottin, pyramide* and *fromages frais.'*

'Obviously you love the countryside too, but do you like goats?' I ask.

'Oh, I love them! They are such gentle creatures. Contrary to people's perception of them they are in fact fragile animals. They are very affectionate and need company. In the spring when the weather is warmer, I take them for a walk on the hills with the dog.'

'Don't they wander away?' I ask.

'Oh no, they like the human contact, they stay together and walk with and all around me. We've got over sixty hectares of land here that we use, thirty five of which are ours and thirty we rent. So we've got plenty of space to wander.'

For nearly twenty-five years Marc and Francoise have lived here, keeping goats and making goat's cheese, known as *fromage de chèvre*.

Their routine is disciplined and they share the work load, they tell me proudly.

'We <u>both</u> do everything, we share all the responsibilities. We take turns at cooking, and looking after the house and we both look after the goats and make the cheese.'

Françoise makes the cheese in the mornings whilst Marc tends the goats and does the milking which is by machine. In the afternoon the jobs are reversed; Marc is to be found in the cheese dairy and Françoise with her beloved goats. She took me to meet them and it was obvious that they love her. Each one has a name and they come when called.

'How do you recognise which is which?'

'Oh, it's just like children – they have different features, it's easy.' And she calls out a name; it's an old grandmother who comes trotting over for a pat and a head scratch. She pokes her shaggy head through the bars of a gate and pushes her muzzle into my hand, her tongue rasps against my palm, it's uncomfortable and I pull my hand away.

Francoise laughs.

'She wants some milk. When the grandmothers grow old they still give a little milk but we feed it back to them. They love it. She thinks you are going to give her some.'

I try to count them in the pen but they're moving about the whole time, reaching for the hay that's stacked around the edges of the enclosure. Françoise sees me and calls out.

'We've got forty-seven at the moment but we've had as many as ninety. Marc is beginning to think about retiring in the not too distant future and so we're keeping the number down.'

'What about the winter? Do they stay indoors?'

'Yes, it can be cold up here. We are 250 metres above sea level and though we don't get much snow, we do get closed in by icy conditions sometimes.'

We can hear Marc calling. It's his turn to start making the cheese and I have been invited to watch the process. I am kitted out with white shoes, cotton coat and a '*charlotte*'; a little white mobcap. As Marc begins to ladle out the milk he explains the process.

'It's in five stages: first adding the rennet to curdle the milk within a period of twenty-four hours. The coagulated milk is then ladled into containers pierced with holes to allow the whey to run off. The blancmange-like shape is then turned out of its small pot and salted with pure salt from the river *Guérande,* or with salted ash. The fourth step is to allow it to dry; the resulting cheeses are placed in a ventilated area where the surface water is made to evaporate by the air currents. Finally comes the *affinage*; the maturing of the cheese.

After the placing of the cheeses on the racks in the drying cabinet – in effect a cool-room – they are turned daily. At eight days they are soft and slightly acidic and at two weeks are firmer and begin to form a crust, when the specific goat's cheese flavour begins to appear. At four weeks the cheese has a stronger flavour, it has dried and breaks apart easily.

This process goes on day in day out during the months of February to November. A nanny goat produces up to 600 litres of milk during this period, 2 or 3 litres of milk a day though at first the milk is reserved for the rearing of the kids; then later is used for making the cheese.

'We don't make cheese in the autumn obviously, during their non-lactating period from November to January,' Marc explains, 'we respect the animal's natural cycle and of course the seasons.'

I am curious as to what they are fed in order to produce such good quality milk. It's partly the natural food available on the hills; oak leaves, junipers, aromatic herbs, specific grasses, and the fine hay gathered from the slopes of La Gard'Haute.

'Our goats are fed nothing but the best,' boasts Marc. 'They have a portion of barley, and a portion of maize at each milking session, morning and evening. This regime guarantees a healthy and natural diet.'

No wonder that Marc and Françoise have won numerous prizes for their high quality goat's cheese. The diplomas and certificates are proudly displayed in the cheese shop adjacent to the dairy. But you can also buy their produce at the market at Pressac on a Friday, or on a Tuesday at Puy l'Eveque.

I prefer to wend my way through the vines and the oaks, even risk getting lost, in order to visit La Gard'Haute and buy their *cabecou* – the little round, soft white discs, for which incidentally (as with their other cheeses too) there are strict rules with regard to its production. It's a treat to visit Marc and Françoise, any afternoon, any day of the week.

If you want to be certain of buying specific cheeses, telephone beforehand:

05 65 36 50 03 but they are hardly ever absent. The goats need their attention, and their company!

Françoise and Marc have a leaflet of recipes using goat's cheese. I can recommend the following which they gave me permission to reproduce here.

Tarte au fromage de chèvre frais

Soft goat's cheese tart

Ingredients

3 soft white goat's cheeses

300 gr of sweet shortcrust pastry

2 dl crème fraîche

4 eggs

200 gr of sugar

2 soup spoons of flour

Method

Roll out the pastry and line a tin to make a pastry case.

Mix in a bowl: the cheese, sugar, flour and salt.

Add the crème fraîche and the well-beaten eggs.

Pour the mixture into the pastry case and cook for 45 mins in a warm oven until the top is golden brown.

Serve warm or cold.

Tomates farcies au chèvre frais

Stuffed tomatoes with goat's cheese

Ingredients

3 soft white goat's cheeses

2 hard boiled eggs

3 coffee spoons of crème fraîche

1 coffee spoon of mustard

1 coffee spoon of lemon juice

1 coffee spoon of paprika

Method

Carefully cut the top off each tomato and take the flesh out of the tomato skin. Salt the insides.

Crush the hard boiled eggs in a bowl, add the cheese, crème fraîche, mustard, lemon juice and paprika, add salt if desired.

Upturn the empty tomato skins to pour off any liquid. Fill with the egg mixture and replace the 'hats'. Serve on a bed of lettuce.

Le Rocamadour en feuilletage au miel

Rocamadour goat's cheese in puff pastry

Ingredients

1 pack of premade puff pastry

Free running honey

Rocamadour cheeses

1 egg – beaten

Method

Roll out the pastry and cut several circles 8 cm in diameter.

Place an individual cheese in the centre of a pastry circle and slightly moisten the edge with water. Place a second layer of pastry over the top taking care to seal the edges.

Snip a small opening in the top with a pair of scissors and gently baste with the beaten egg.

Cook in a warm oven until the pastry is crisp.

Just before serving spoon a little liquid honey over the top and into the hole in the lid.

Serve warm.

This is my version of the goat's cheese salad which you can find on almost every menu in the south west of France.

La salade au fromage de chèvre chaud

Warm goat's cheese salad

Ingredients

Green Salad – leaves of your own choice, and there's plenty to choose from!

Small goat's cheeses

Lardons (chunks of smoked bacon or ham)

Walnut pieces

1 baguette or other bread

Olive Oil

Dressing

Method

Prepare the green salad in your own way which will be divided between the number of portions required.

Mix a dressing of your choice – vinaigrette or a variation of your choice – though the simpler the better.

Fry gently in olive oil the required number of small rounds of a sliced baguette, or you can toast them if you prefer.

Fry some *lardons*, (small chunks of smoked bacon or ham) until fairly crisp.

Place a small *cabecou,* (a thin round goat's cheese) on each piece of fried bread and then place under the grill for a few minutes, until the cheese begins to melt.

Add the dressing, fried lardons and a handful of walnuts to the salad and mix well.

Divide the salad between the plates and place one or two 'toasts' on top of the salad.

If you wish to make this salad a little bit more special and traditional, you can mix in some pieces of cooked duck. In France it is usually *gésiers* that is used, the little bits and pieces other than main sections such as breast or leg; the French don't waste any morsel of meat from the duck! But you can use whatever you fancy.

Epilogue

The writing of 'French Impressions' took longer than I had anticipated. The book came about as a record of my feelings about the countryside of this particular area of the south west of France where I have had a house for some years.

As I travelled around exploring mediaeval towns and villages, visiting museums, going to the markets, and just enjoying the scenery, I realised that it was the people too who made this place what it is. So I began my quest to learn more of the region by talking to the ordinary, everyday people of the area.

In the Introduction I quote;

'Connaitre une region, c'est connaitre la vie des gens qui l'ont batie'- to get to know a region first one must get to know the people who have built it.

That's when I set out to interview interesting people I met in the market, in the villages, in restaurants, my neighbours and friends.

I speak French moderately well, even so, some of the interviews were difficult. There is a strong regional accent which at times made comprehension difficult.

Then came the translation of what I had recorded. All of this took time, longer than I had foreseen. Taking photographs was also a time consuming undertaking; trying to capture the essence of a place with a camera is much harder than one at first thinks, but I hope my pictures do it justice.

As I get to know this area more and more, my love of it continues to grow.

As we set off on the long journey by car from southern England for another visit, I get butterflies in my tummy in anticipation of our arrival at our French home. The flutter of excitement intensifies as I near our house. It surprises me that after all these years the excitement on arrival is still there.

I hope it never fades.

The End